Enough
Is
Enough.

Enough Is enough.

YES, YOU'RE IN A RELATIONSHIP WITH A NARCISSIST! — THE 32 UNDENIABLE SIGNS YOU'RE IN A TOXIC NARCISSISTIC RELATIONSHIP AND HOW TO STEP-BY-STEP GET ON THE PATH OF NARCISSISTIC ABUSE RECOVERY

CHRISTINE MURRAY

BODY MIND &SPIRIT
B O O K S

First Edition

Edited by Rodney Miles, www.RodneyMiles.com

"Frame Mirror Picture" (opposite title page and flourish) © Pixabay.com

Chapter quotes © BrainyQuote.com

For Alex, Tiffany, Andrew, and Jeannie

Truth is like surgery. It hurts but it cures. A lie is like a pain killer. It gives instant relief. But has side effects forever.

—Unknown

CONTENTS

INTRODUCTION

"Narcissus was a hunter in Greek mythology, son of the river god Cephissus and the nymph Liriope. He was a very beautiful young man, and many fell in love with him. However, he only showed them disdain and contempt."

—www.greekmythology.com

I AM NOT a psychologist nor an academic. I am an intelligent, now independent woman who has survived a horrible experience with who I am well-convinced was and is a person with Narcissistic Personality Disorder (for the rest of the book we will call them "NPDs"), and I have learned so much about what happened (and when it's over, that's when you start looking back, figuring out *what happened*). My purpose is purely to help others avoid, detect, handle, and get out of situations and relationships such as I was victim to. I am not just looking out for you. I am looking out for those you love—kids, spouse, friends, family.

I am looking out for the lost opportunities and human potential involved. No one ever seems to talk about that, but when someone is stuck in a relationship with an NPD, just like when a cult gets a hold of a *good person,* the contributions that person might have made are stolen from the society. It's a bit broader view, for sure, but it's true enough. Meanwhile, if you have picked up this book, I'm sure you are simply trying to figure out *what the hell is going on, and how you handle it.*

I was invalidated, subjugated, physically abused, isolated socially and without true friends or career, and abandoned without help or money with my four children in Costa Rica *by my husband.* Only then did I start to realize it was up to me to start waking up, to start taking actions on my own to determine our destinies—mine and that of my kids. I did it, too, and I don't want any of that to happen to you, so I have written this book.

I was in an abusive relationship with "an NPD" and it cost me dearly. It cost me *years* of undervaluing myself, years of confusion, nagging fear and insecurity, years of not pursuing my actual, underlying dreams, years of neglecting and in fact denying my natural talents and interests. I did recognized it "one day," and I did something about it, *finally,* almost too late. Part of my years of living with it was the fact that no one around me seemed to tell me, even though in retrospect, they *had to know* I was in a lousy relationship.

So what changed?

My kids, that's what. We had four children together and I shiver to look back at the times I considered a "morning after" pill, considered leaving both my husband and my kids—but one does not know quite what is wrong *until one knows what is wrong!* So here's a little good news for you. If you've picked this book up, you may or might not be in a relationship—whether with a lover, co-worker, family member, or friend— with a person who "suffers" NPD, but even if you are, I can tell you first-hand *there are good things that can come out of even these relationships.*

One of those things is understanding, one is grit and determination if you've been fighting through it all these years, and another might be *children.* My four kids are the biggest blessings in my life today and I finally see them free of the clouded lens of a relationship with a narcissist.

You can be free of that, too, and I'm here to tell you, the sun does shine clearly again. Your heart can be free again. And shit—you can even live to laugh about it all, once it's all clear and safely *behind you.*

This book is for people who suspect that their partner or another close to them is a narcissist. This book will go over how to understand narcissists, recognize narcissists, and get on the path of recovery from narcissistic abuse. And by the end you will be able to do all of these things, quite naturally. It will steel you to them for the rest of your life, and you will be able to help others as well.

The mirror icon I use at all chapter starts is to remind us with each new chapter both that the narcissist and the more severe case of the NPD are wholly concerned with themselves, even if you are near them, just as Narcissus was in the old myth. It is also there to remind us with each chapter that perhaps new journey for us is to *discover* who we are, anew, because we can never go back, we are now more experienced versions of ourselves, and I will talk about my journey to rediscover myself, in new and exciting ways, to be honest.

The quotes at the beginning of each chapter I've selected based on whether or not they illuminate some part of this subject *for me,* in the perhaps self-centered idea that if they have helped me, they will help you.

If you're like me, there are times I suspect and fear something is true, only to kind of get chills when I see the symptoms described by another. You don't *want* your narcissistic person to be a narcissistic person, and that's part of the denial. And I've also found good people have a hard time believing or understanding when others are not also driven by good intentions. It's confusing. But if there's confusion it does not mean it's *yours,* necessarily. You can be sensing something there that is not a part of you, something that is in the environment, or in someone else.

While I call on lots of memories with my ex-husband, it turns out I've known several narcissists in my life. One hint came from, believe it or not, a psychic! It started out weird and ended up profound. I ended up in a conversation with a locally well-known professional psychic outside a shopping center one day. As we talked, not one but two people stopped to say hello to her, one saying even though it had been a while he needed to see her. She seemed to like me and she asked if I'd like a reading. I hesitated, but said, "Sure!"

We sat on a bench and she looked at my hands. She explained that the people I thought were my friends were really not, that they were actually *jealous* of me. I was kind of shocked, because it explained so much! I had an *uneasy and sort of confused* feeling about these friends—two in particular I was spending a lot of time with—and what she said explained a lot. Now, all these years later, in looking back, one in particular clearly suffers from Narcissistic Personality Disorder (NPD).

I hope you will have similar "ah-has" throughout your read. I have tried to combine and balance my own anecdotal personal stories with research. When you become aware of something you *become aware of it,* and it really takes no effort at all to then simply see it when it exists. The simple game of "Punch Buggy" serves perfectly here. Once you become aware of a car model they seem to magically appear all over the roads. So it is when you can readily detect and handle the NPD.

Once you are familiar with the traits that suggest *narcissism* or even Narcissistic Personality Disorder (NPD), things—self-protection, better relationships, even *self*-evaluation and easier thoughts, emotions, and behaviors, and happiness—become *easier.* For example, while going down the list of nine traits that indicate NPD (in this book) my new partner and I kind of laughed and rolled our eyes as he and I rea each one in turn and said, "Ah-huh! Bill!" or "Mom *and* Dad," and so on. It's not a joke, but *everyone* has some of these, sometimes, and for me, I felt a maybe weird sense of relief at seeing how both my mother and father had a lot of these traits and might even be well-described as narcissists! It makes sense of certain things.

The traits alone do not a narcissist make, as Shouten and Silver say, *the severity* if the traits is what makes or doesn't make a narcissist or a psychopath.

And seeing the traits in my mother and father now does not make me fear or love them less, it helps me understand them, and it helps me understand *me*. The recognition and acceptance helps me detach from being a slave to the traits, *frees me from them*. I feel *cleaner,* I feel rational, I feel *sane,* I feel *happy,* and I feel *free*.

You can, too.

PART 1:
UNDERSTANDING

[1] INSANITY RISING

"I am a recovering narcissist. I thought narcissism was about self-love till someone told me there is a flip side to it. It is actually drearier than self-love; it is unrequited self-love."

—Emily Levine

MENTAL ILLNESS—in fact, *insanity*—is, according to Donald Capps in *Understanding Psychosis,* on the rise over the last 250 years. He notes that rates of insanity are higher in urban areas than rural areas. And in modern society, he states:

> "I am not yet willing to forego the theory that a significant reason for the increase of insanity over the years is is the 'over-exertion of the mind' or

'vulnerable minds being overwhelmed by the extra work needed to handle [life's] complexity.' . . . a typical precondition of psychosis is a combination of significant levels of vulnerability and stress. This would seem to support the idea that the increase in psychotic illness is due, at least in part, to the pressures placed on vulnerable minds to deal with life's complexities (Capps, 23)."

And life is getting more complex, for sure.

I didn't see it that way until a boss while speaking to a group of us remarked that "computers and electronics are supposed to make easier, but what they really do is give us more to do." I'd add to that the fact that as the world intermingles more and more, cultures are melding together, violence seems to be on the rise, and despite all of the "safe spaces" and turning from abusive parenting, childhood seems as complex as ever. I do believe, as historians will attest, that civilization is getting ever less violent, but that seems to bely the *new* complexities and uncertainties of life today. Sometimes, we can't see what we're living through, as we're too close and don't yet have the benefit of hindsight and it's perhaps, a subject for a whole additional period of thought, research, and books.

For some strange reason, given my experiences with narcissists, I perhaps selfishly find comfort in the idea that *narcissism* in particular seems to be on the rise. I'm also appalled and worried by it, but there's something that says *I'm not crazy!* when you find out others have gone through this, too. And there's something personally comforting to know what has ailed you is ailing others everywhere. That, of course, is the selfish view, but when you're stuck under something heavy you are innately "selfish" for a little while, to say the least. And the analogy, while it might be extreme and funny, is maybe more fitting than you at first realize.

So in researching this book, I found numbers that suggest NPD itself is on the rise. All well and good, but what hit more closely to home was finding a resource new (to me) at Quora. A woman named Veronica who started a page there, in the space where you describe your page, *apologizes* for no longer being able to maintain the page due to rapid and unexpected growth of the chat regarding narcissism and narcissists! Here's the page, and I recommend it:

https://www.quora.com/q/narcissism-narcissists

THE SIGNS AROUND US

There have been things in the past that didn't sit right with me in the behavior of others and in myself, too, to be honest. I noticed them as life rolled along, and now, with my newfound knowledge of narcissists and Narcissistic Personality Disorder (NPD), when I look back they seem to make sense. For example, two people—may father and a close friend—seemed to *always* send food back when we went to restaurants. They seemed to *always* be condescending and rude or mean to servers at restaurants as well. It got so bad with them that my significant other and I decided to stop eating out with them, ever.

Today I recognize this as a symptom of narcissism. I don't mean sending food back means you're a narcissist, I mean *always sending book back, almost ritualistically, and always being an ass to servers* is for me, a red flag. I used to judge people on how they treated servers, cashiers, and the like—people in positions where they cannot readily speak back or stand up for themselves. I regarded it as condescending, rude, arrogant, stupid and cruel, but today I see it as a little string that if pulled will likely reveal a greater personality disorder.

And I have begun standing up for people subjected to these unfair attacks. In fact, recently on a cruise, I told another passenger who was being incredibly rude to a staff member that they were being an a—hole to the person trying to serve them, that they were preoccupied with "first world problems," and they should be grateful or keep their mouth shut. The person I told this too looked shocked and walked away. I think I was just as surprised—I couldn't believe I said that.

As you get versed with the terms and facts of personality disorders, in our case here, *narcissism,* you are more enabled and secure in your convictions, and you might surprise yourself at how easy it becomes to have integrity and to also protect those around you better, if you so choose.

Fast forward and I'm desperate to improve my family's situation, living in almost unbearable conditions, and again, desperate to try *anything* to make things work for me, my husband, and our four little kids. In economic desperation, I have the idea that we'll move to Costa Rica. The cost of living is less, the pictures make it look like a land of tropical forests and beaches, and a volcano, even. Maybe I can transform our violent struggle as a family into something many dream of. Maybe with a much lower cost of living, I can continue with school and live on the grants and loans until I have something better to offer the world. Maybe my husband will get motivated, get off the couch, and maybe less stress will inspire him to be the kinder man I knew a few years ago.

Wishful thinking is natural and gets a lot of us further down a bad road than we ever thought we'd go.

We *did* become expatriates, we did move to Costa Rica, and while the beauty and the challenges were pretty much as expected, the change in environment did no good in altering my NPD's psychology. It was even more frustrating because of that. The arguments grew. The kids' situation became more dangerous and uncertain. The sexual and physical assaults on me began again—I was sick in my head, heart, and stomach that things were reverting back to the old ways I sought to escape and solve with such a major life change.

But I might have remained, had the violence not started to get directed at my children, had the carelessness (lack of care, lack of empathy) not extended to my kids. And when I finally heard from my visiting sister that he had gotten surprisingly violent with Alex, our oldest, I might have never woken up. No one else seemed to care. No one else—not our new pastor, our new friends, the people at church—seemed to say anything to me at all about what they must have witnessed. Only my sister.

Today I understand that was all by design and by advantage. NPDs isolate, and the move to CR might have been just what my ex needed to keep us from the truth, to keep us in his fish bowl.

So, *what the hell happened?* What the hell is wrong with a person that *this* is their plan for life, for their own family? It seems to make no sense at all. At least not until you start looking instead of wishing, start to read instead of believe, to consider things don't have to be this way.

I considered jumping into this book at this point with a list of red flags, of symptoms of NPDs. After all, that's what I'm so eager to convey—tools you can use right away and get on with a better life, or perhaps in some cases, *save your life.*

Understand, Recognize,

Decide

But let's back up a bit and try to understand what the NPD is going through. That's not to say compassion for the NPD comes first—*it does not.* Trying to help or salvage your own NPD might be like it was with mine, more on the order of pulling a violent bull out of a ditch when the safety and sanity of you and your children are at risk. **You have to find safety and sanity for yourself first.** And the truth is, you might never be able to help them. You might, but you might not. In either case, it's usually safer to get free of them first, if only for bargaining if not to save lives and minds. And it will all make more sense when we understand the NPD better, believe me.

This section, "Part 1: Understanding," will have some things in common with "Part 2: Recognizing," but that's intentional. The main difference is the intention. In this, Part 1, we are starting to understand the theory behind what makes an NPD tick. In Part 2, we'll continue that study, but with more of an eye for detecting the red flags when they go up. I will say again, as I will many times throughout this book, it's not the simple presence alone of indications, behaviors, symptoms—whatever you might like to call them, it's the *regularity* and the *severity* of the symptoms that makes an actual NPD. For our purposes, we should become familiar with the probable causes for understanding, the common symptoms for recognizing them, and the proven solutions—at least for *us,* if not the NPDs themselves.

Today I have NPDs around me I understand, accept, and am ready to deal with, for all their faults. And there are others I avoid like a plague. I am happier, healthier, saner, and safer for it.

[2] PERSONALITY DISORDERS

"Narcissism falls along the axis of what psychologists call personality disorders . . . But by most measures, narcissism is one of the worst, if only because the narcissists themselves are so clueless."

—Jeffrey Kluger

We should start our look at NPDs with an understanding of what we are looking for. As Komrad says:

> "There are three major expressions of mental life: *thoughts, feelings,* and *behaviors.* You can think of these as the three legs of a stool. A problem or weakening in any one (or more) of these supports will throw off the

stool's balance. In the brain—the seat of mental life—problems with thoughts, feelings or behaviors can lead to suffering and problems functioning. And as you have observed, those problems can also affect those whose lives intersect the life of the troubled person (Komrad)."

So if we break the problem down, we can divide our observation into looking into these three things:

1. Thought
2. Feelings
3. Behaviors

And in fact, as you will see when we discuss treatment (when it can be applied at all), those are the three areas we treat.

CLUSTER B

There is a category of psychological illness disorder called "Cluster B Personality Disorders." Such a person may exhibit irrational behavior and have trouble controlling their emotions, all of which can cause problems in life, problems with relationships, at work and so on. "A personality disorder is a mental health condition that affects the way a person thinks, behaves, and relates to other people" (Burgess).

It helps to look at what are consider the A, B, and C of personality disorders:

- **Cluster A**: People diagnosed with cluster A personality disorders may find it hard to relate to others. They may behave in a way that others consider odd, eccentric, or paranoid.

- **Cluster B**: People diagnosed with cluster B personality disorders may find it hard to regulate their emotions. This may cause relationship problems. They may behave in a way that others consider overly emotional, dramatic, or erratic.

- **Cluster C**: People diagnosed with cluster C personality disorders may be seen by others as antisocial or withdrawn. They may feel very anxious and behave in a fearful manner. (Burgess)

And within Cluster B there are four types of disorders:

1. Antisocial
2. Borderline
3. Histrionic

4. Narcissistic

(Burgess)

The person afflicted with any of these can have a disruptive, disturbing effect upon those around them.

Someone with **Antisocial Personality Disorder** may act in a way that suggests they do not care about other people's needs. They might lie, cheat or trick, and deceive others, all apparently to their own benefit. They might be aggressive, impulsive, irresponsible, and even aggressive toward others. They usually lack empathy and show no regret or worry about their actions.

Someone with **Borderline Personality Disorder** may have a low and fragile self-esteem, to the point that it affects how they relate to and deal with other people. They often fear abandonment or being left alone, paranoid, and empty. This causes them emotional stress and of course, adversely affects their relationships. The slightest things can cause them to feel angry or sad, things that might not really bother other people, and these reactions are often seen as manipulative. These people often have suicidal thoughts and tendencies or can be prone to self-harm.

Someone with **Histrionic Personality Disorder** may seem to always be seeking attention, often inappropriately. They can be overly emotional and even sexually provocative, dramatic, and to have strong, often unsupported opinions. They sometimes act as if they are closer to people than they actually are, and they too can tend to be suicidal or prone to self-harm.

Someone with **Narcissistic Personality Disorder** seems to think they are superior to others, react too harshly to criticism, have larger-than-life plans and ideas, crave admiration, feel highly entitled, and lack empathy for others. And they seem (or are) manipulative of those around them

We might all at one time or another exhibit some of these traits, so if you are sitting there reading thinking, *Oh no!* with regard to yourself, take a breath because self-reflection is not something people with such disorders typically thrive on..

DIAGNOSIS

But if you're interested—and you should be, actually—in what a proper diagnosis takes—and many a personality disorder sufferer *will* actually sit long enough for evaluation in the self-interest of a better life, as difficult as narcissists can be—diagnosis is accomplished according to the guidelines set forth in what is (currently) titled, *The Diagnostic and Statistical Manual of Mental Disorders, Fifth Edition* or *DSM-5*. After breaking personality disorders into the three categories or "clusters" discussed (A, B, C), it further describes specific symptoms which suggest a diagnosis of a cluster B personality disorder.

To diagnose, a licensed professional will confidentially discuss with a person their thoughts, feelings, behavior, and their life with them. They will discuss their relationships. Specific symptoms which must be present for a clinical diagnosis of cluster B personality disorder include:

- Traits first appeared when a person was an adolescent or young adult
- If over 18, traits have persisted for greater than a year
- Traits must seem consistent over time and in different circumstances
- Traits must be the likely cause of distress that negatively affect the person's well-being
- These symptoms should not likely be due to another disorder
- Nor should they be attributable to only an isolated, stressful situation (Burgess).

THE WOUND THAT NEVER HEALS

People with NPD *seem to* see themselves as clearly and naturally superior to others, to the degree they are only "happy" when demonstrating control over others. The appearance of self-confidence, arrogance, egomania, and condescension is actually what masks "deep-seated insecurity and lack of self-esteem." It makes sense in that context that they would then crave and depend upon attention, praise, and recognition of their superiority indeed to validate what they are insisting upon, but ironically, deeply unsure of. It also explains a quick and deep sensitiveness to rejection and invalidation (Alta Mira). These are often met with great fury or obsessive thoughts and acts of revenge, whether overt or subtle.

Believe me, I know, and if you're reading this book, I bet you know it, too.

So underneath it all is tremendous tension, a constant battle for deeply doubted self-esteem and worth, eased seemingly only by a regular state of submission and praise by others. It's exhausting for everyone, believe me, even the narcissist, if you ask me. Narcissists can constantly feel misunderstood and undervalued, while also frantically hiding the fact that their confidence and superiority is really a façade, a fraud.

[3] NARCISSISM

"If we weren't born with anti-social passions - narcissism, envy, lust, meanness, greed, hunger for power, just to name the more obvious - why the need for so many laws, whether religious or secular, that govern behavior?"

—Dennis Prager

A PET PEEVE

I am a survivor. I use these terms with care, such as *narcissist,* or person afflicted with Narcissistic Personality Disorder, which we refer to as an "NPD" in this book. In my own case, my ex-husband as far I know, to this day has never subjected himself to diagnosis or treatment and would vehemently deny or laugh off being any kind of narcissist. This is part of the difficulty in diagnosing, treating, or indeed helping such people in any practical way. In fact, if you ask me, the diagnosis in the case of narcissism is most helpful not in treatment of the *subject* but for use in detection (and avoidance!) by those around him or her, for use by the narcissist's potential or actual victims.

But one of my pet peeves is hearing people toss around terms—serious terms, sometimes—without being careful or trying to at least be exact as they do it. "Narcissism" is one of those that should probably not be tossed around too loosely. Often, it fits someone's narrative to call another a "narcissist" when that other person is simply exhibiting self-interest or taking an opposing view. The consequences are bad. "Racism" is a fine example of this, where if one's ideas are opposed it's kind of a dirty trick to pollute the debate by levying "racist!" when not the case. The importance is that *racism* is in fact a serious thing in not only an argument but in another's worldview, if polluted by such a stupid bias as skin color. In that case, it's important to recognize racism (in this example), but if racism did not play a role in the thinking of your opponent, you muddy the water, you prevent honest and intellectual debate, and you also prevent—most importantly—and honest and mutually beneficial resolution. You prevent any advance in actual understanding and you *dilute* the term "racism" at the same time, so possibly, if and when racism actually applies, it might be ignored or minimalized or in the least, confusing. It's just as simple as when that boy cried "wolf!" one too many times. So, let's not fall for that.

I see the term "narcissist" thrown about to mean, by context, "arrogance" or self-involvement, ego. And that's the basis of the disorder, perhaps, but the disorder goes further, of course. We all have to eat but eat too little (anorexia) or too much and we suffer. In the case of Narcissistic Personality Disorder, it's "sociopathy" because it causes *others* to suffer, it causes others to live in a way that is to some degree and some manner subservient, often only partially knowingly if at all.

Basically, a *narcissist* is someone who places too much importance on themselves, and not enough on others. While they insist on being admired, praised, and served by others, they usually don't bother or are incapable of seeing or caring to see others' point of view. A little narcissism or ego is healthy—you take care of your appearance and cleanliness, for example, and you insist on your own integrity, for example. It's the imbalance of this that gets to be a problem. If one cares too much about their own appearance and has no regard for others this can be unhealthy or even unsafe and might be called "narcissism." Taken to an extreme this can be called *Narcissistic Personality Disorder*.

PERSONALITY DISORDERS

Once we grasp that the term "narcissist" began with Greek mythology, and that in general this is a person over-endowed with self-love (one difference being that our original narcissist died of the grief knowing he was alone, in love with himself), and we differentiate between the street-use of the term being bestowed on anyone with an obvious ego to the more technical use denoting Narcissistic Personality Disorder according to specific criteria, it's useful to know there is a spectrum or range of narcissism. Armed with knowledge we can determine if the people in our lives are just egotistical or if they indeed need to be dealt with carefully or in some cases, not at all (Scott).

A narcissist isn't necessarily a person with Narcissistic Personality Disorder, or NPD. *Personality disorders* are precise, "stable maladaptive patterns of behavior" and according to the American Psychological Association (APA), include at least two of these four maladaptive patterns:

- Cognitive/thought
- Affective/emotional
- Interpersonal/relating to others
- Impulse-control (Scott).

A SPECTRUM

Narcissism is not an absolute, but a range, or *spectrum* of severity. We all need a dash of it—self-love, that is—actually, as in small and appropriate doses we are making an accurate estimation of the environment and our efforts in it, or we go about seeking recompense for honest efforts, we can have integrity, and so on. A bit too much in excess and the world—

laymen and professionals alike—now recognizes a person as a *narcissist*. An in great excess, one might be diagnosed as having Narcissistic Personality Disorder.

Only a trained, and appropriately licensed professional in the field of mental health can make a diagnosis of any personality disorder, including NPD. We "talk science" in this book but the purpose is to develop personal judgement that can lead you to begin to improve your own awareness and ultimately your conditions and situations in life, for you and those you love.

So there is a spectrum and there are different "variants" of narcissism, different types of narcissists, and different degrees of how severe a narcissist one is. Here are a few:

- **Grandiose narcissists** require *lots* of constant praise and attention;
- **Vulnerable narcissists** need lots of support and have lots of anxiety;
- But the worst, most damaging type is clearly the **malignant narcissist**, who instead of simply focus all the time on themselves and demand the admiration of all around them, consistently display the symptoms listed under Narcissistic Personality Disorder along with sadistic and antisocial traits, a poor sense of self, and a lack of empathy. In fact this is closely related to *psychopathy* as they often exhibit these three, key, common traits:

- o Sadism
- o Antisocial behavior
- o Lack of empathy

Malignant narcissists are often very manipulative, without regard for others as long as they get their own way. Others are seen in black and white terms, either friend of foe and in their wake they leave a lot of tragedy behind them—heartache, pain, confusion. But they don't care—in fact they probably enjoy it and feel a sense of power from it, despite how easily they sometimes crumble when they are dealt the same (Scott).

PERSONALITY TYPES

Before we go too much further, I think it's important to again remind ourselves that *all of us* might at times exhibit some of these egotistical traits, and it's important to recognize differences. In fact, for a great resource on different personality types (in the context of how reassuring they can be), see this great article:

"Here's How Reassuring You Can Be, Based on Your Personality Type"

https://personalitygrowth.com/heres-how-reassuring-you-can-be-based-on-your-personality-type/

The article is fascinating, but outside the scope of this book, and while interesting, perhaps not vital if you are seeking a quick understanding and resolution of your relationship with a narcissist.

[4]

CODEPENDENCY

"Whoever loves becomes humble."

—Sigmund Freud

YOU'VE PROBABLY HEARD the term, *co-dependency*, and maybe even imagined what it means. If you're in an actual state of co-dependency, you might also be in a bit of denial, if we're being honest and blunt. At the same time, *I understand*—remember, I've been there! And I commend you now for looking into this more deeply. You should definitely understand what we mean by "co-dependent."

Simply, it's an *emotional* state, and one that tells you to "stay," that you cannot leave because your survival in some way depends upon it.

And that's what NPDs want.

I can tell you to stop it, but that won't work until you yourself *decide* you *have* stopped it and you're moving on. Often, necessity gets us to do that, and in some cases, only greater destruction and even death will end a co-dependent relationship. But I can tell you, the healthiest way to get through and over one is to do it yourself, before it's too late, and the way you start that proves is with what you're doing—reading, looking, thinking, being honest with yourself.

Co-dependency is considered learned behavior and something we pass down through generations, possibly. It's both an emotional and a behavioral issue, sometimes called "relationship addiction" (Mental Health America). Maybe you've known someone or been in a relationship where breaking seemed like a horrible and feared possibility.

I had first-hand experience with a co-dependent relationship early on, but I didn't learn from it as much as I should have. Amy (not her real name) met Bill (nor his) when she was the family nanny and they began a sexual relationship. *And who knew it wouldn't last!* Amy became pregnant and they had a beautiful daughter and seemed to get along most of the time pretty well. After a while, Bill started drinking regularly, they fought violently, and even to a point once where he hit her and she *stabbed* him. It as one night after they had been fighting quite a bit, early on in their marriage that I pulled them aside, confident I could help them. The result was Bill standing up and saying very matter-of-factly. "Amy, I just don't want to be with you anymore." And he left. I took Amy to Denny's where we ate Grand Slam Breakfasts and I listened to her, quite amazed when it hit me she intended to *stay* in the relationship.

For twenty years (literally) I advised Amy to leave Bill—when the fights upset the kids, when he refused to stop drinking, when he cheated multiple times on her—and her regular answer was, "That's *my man*." The behavior, the viewpoint, was likely learned to mimic or in response to what *she* saw as a child in her home, which I understood was pretty rough a well.

When Bill did finally leave Amy, he had to trick her into it (seriously). He explained to her the only shot their relationship had was to go through with a divorce, to see if they still loved each other outside of marriage. And she agreed to try. She was heartbroken as Bill went off to the opposite coast and started a new relationship, but not before Amy destroyed any remaining self-respect by following Bill around, yelling outside of hotel rooms, horrifying her now teenage daughter with her irrational behavior.

The only thing that made any sense to me for a long time was that Amy had, for whatever reasons, practically no self-respect in the first place, and that she considered she depended on Bill completely, economically. But it was more than that. Bill offered and sent her money to try an assuage her through their breakup, but it took *years* for Amy to reach a point where she could hold a job, not sleep in her car or on a friend's couch or go an hour without breaking down into tears. And she did seek help in ways, she checked into an institution at one point, and God knows what else.

I didn't really know how to help Amy. I tried to warn her all those years ago, but I was up against *co-dependency*. She had the idea (and maybe still does) that she could not survive and was not worth anything of value without Bill.

But she is!

If I know it, she does not.

I tell this obviously as a cautionary tale. Amy stayed in a relationship that was "one-sided, emotionally destructive, and/or abusive." The condition and the term originated during research just years ago into the families of alcoholics, and the behavior is generally agreed to arise out of watching other family members do the same. Co-dependency is said to rise out of *dysfunctional families,* defined by the existence of possible underlying problems:

- A family member addicted to drugs, sex, gambling, alcohol, or even food
- Abuse, whether physical, sexual, or psychological
- A family member with a mental disorder or physical illness (Mental Health America).

The first thing to know about dysfunctional families is that they *do not acknowledge that problems exist.* They do not confront them or even talk about them.

And that gives you the first step to fixing one, doesn't it?

In Amy's case, she sacrificed many important things to be with Bill, and once he had left her, she felt a weird and vast sense of entitlement with no satisfaction (as perhaps she should have, but it was unreasonable and futile to expect people other than Bill to make up for it. It cost her friendships and squandered—at least for a period of years—her real potential, as well as her potential for happiness, which I am sure she had plenty.

Placing all their hopes and dreams in the hands of another, often mentally-ill or abusive other, co-dependents can "lose themselves," seemingly completely. They are usually good people, but they are most guilty of neglecting themselves in these ways described and slip into an apparent complete loss of self-esteem.

I should know!

It has taken me *years* to arrive at writing about this in a book! But I have grown that much in confidence, using the techniques we have yet to cover.

There is an excellent article here:

https://www.mentalhealthamerica.net/co-dependency

Please do check it out for the list of characteristics and the questionnaire if you have any idea that you or someone you know might be a co-dependent in a toxic way. For our purposes, let's get back to our discussion of narcissists, now that we have seen the obvious role co-dependency plays in attaching a victim to an NPD.

[5] CAUSES & TREATMENT

"One thing a narcissist doesn't like is to look in a mirror that is in any way genuinely reflective of what's on the other side of it."

—Jay Parini

CAUSES

CAUSES ARE NOT *definitely* known, by any means, but it is *believed* that both environmental and genetic factors play a role in causing and creating personality disorders. In particular, studies suggest sexual trauma, childhood verbal abuse, a certain type of brain development, and a family history contribute (Burgess). According to studies, it is believed that over 25 percent of NPD sufferers are narcissists due to genetic factors, with environmental factors creating the other 75 percent, notably, "dysfunctional parent-child-relationships." We can lump certain situations into this category. *Overly demanding, authoritarian* parents who create environments where a child feels like nothing is ever good enough for the parent(s), and where the child is then encouraged to overcompensate and adopt narcissistic attitudes and practices is one scenario believed to create narcissists. *Inconsistent parents* is another, where boundaries are either never established and a child swings between indulgence to neglect. A child can thereby get deeply confused, and "escape" into a self-created fantasy world. And of course, for the child, *emotional, physical, and sexual abuse* can devastate a child's fragile and developing self-esteem. It can do the same for anyone at the hands of abuse from another, whether a caregiver, teacher, family member, or anyone for that matter (Alta Mira).

TREATMENT

NPDs seem particularly incapable of seeing their own disorder or the damage they cause. In the field of mental illness, this is called *anosognosia*—everyone except the afflicted person can see the problem! That's why people with NPD are sure it's not them but *everyone else* that has a problem! It causes untold stress for family members, loved ones, associates, and it makes them hard to diagnose, much less treat. As Komrad points out, "*They don't think anything is wrong with them* (Komrad, 59)." All sorts of wild behavior can be a result of this but this aspect is one of the most important for victims to understand when it comes to the NPD (Komrad).

So while Narcissistic Personality Disorder is usually very resistant to therapy or other treatments, but there does exist a range of treatments available for cluster B personality disorders (of which Narcissistic Personality Disorder is one), depending on the individual and their circumstances. To determine the best possible route for therapy, a doctor trained in these diagnoses and methods is always recommended. In our case, this technical discussion helps us better understand the symptoms and there severity of what it is we might be dealing with in our spouse, family member or friend, work associate, or another close to us.

According to the latest medial and psychological practices, there are four main methods of treatment for personality disorders, but in my experience, the person afflicted with NPD is unlikely to recognize they have any problem, and perhaps less likely to agree to any kind of treatment at all. Therein lies the difficulty, and there is why my strongest recommendation (spoiler alert!) in this book is to *leave*. And as we'll see, "leaving" might not be an instantaneous thing, but a runway or a process, and perhaps, in the case of children, for example, never fully, absolutely attainable. In that case, *distance in time and space* is my strongest personal recommendation, as we'll discuss.

But as I mentioned, each is a unique case, and understanding the science now behind the diagnosis can be incredibly helpful.

The four main paths of therapy include:

- Talk therapy
- Cognitive behavioral therapy (CBT)
- Dialectical behavior therapy (DBT)
- Medication

Talk therapy, or perhaps better known as simply *psychotherapy,* involves a patient talking freely about their thoughts and feelings in a safe, private space and in a confidential manner with a trained therapist who listens, makes non-judgmental determinations, and offers advice.

In **cognitive behavioral therapy** a person's thought patterns are examined so they can be evaluated and changed in practical ways.

With **dialectical behavioral therapy** a person learns new skills designed to assist in their making their own positive changes in their ways of thinking and behaving, in their relationships, and in life.

And when it comes to **medication** (drugs), there are none specifically designed for personality disorders, but such things as mood stabilizers, antipsychotics, antidepressants, and antianxiety medications might help improve a person's symptoms, if by virtue of aiding with other related disorders that might exacerbate the person's condition, like anxiety or depression (Burgess).

DRUGS AND ALCOHOL

Drugs and alcohol often help ease this constant state of inner panic—at least they seem to, even if temporarily, making recreational drugs and alcohol less valuable or even dangerous as attempted remedies. Addiction can easily take over in these cases.

Drug and alcohol addiction rates in the U.S. are at all-time highs, and more people suffer from NPD than you might be aware.

- It's estimated that more than 6 percent of all adult Americans suffer NPD (men more than women, for whatever it's worth).
- Over 21 percent of those with NPD demonstrate symptoms of alcohol abuse, which is much higher than "most people," nearly *four times* as much.
- Over 9 percent of those with NPD show signs of drug addiction, about 3.5 times higher than with most people.

So giving them drugs and alcohol is probably not a good idea, even if they are not already users themselves. And the data above goes further and suggests a correlation between drug and alcohol abuse and NPD. Treatment might require addressing both the NPD and the addiction, at the same time (Alta Mira).

The NPD is suffering "a wound that never heals." As a result, use of drugs and alcohol to temporarily tune out the constant strain can easily slip into dependency, which can exacerbate the bad behavior (mental and physical abuse), and sooner or later end up in overdose. And overdose is serious stuff for the patient. Over 64,000 Americans die every year from drug overdose, and another 2,000 from alcohol poisoning, not to mention the extended damage NPDs do to their victims in drug and alcohol-induced states (Alta Mira).

CANNABIS AND NPD

It's about at this point in thinking many of us will wonder what *cannabis* or *marijuana* might offer in helping your narcissist. To be blunt, I'm of the opinion, *not much*. In fact even though I'm a personal proponent of medical cannabis properly recommended by a trained physician (rather than simply saying "Smoke away!" in the vein of "treatment") but there are certain diagnoses and conditions that I simply believe do not lend themselves to therapy, treatment, and other methods of relief the rest of us might find helpful.

People with NPD, while constantly and all costs maintaining an appearance of superiority, are believed to be stricken by stress and anxiety beneath it all, driving it all, even. This theory then suggests that the common use of drugs and alcohol by narcissists is one way they deal with the stress, especially when their stress is at high levels. In fact, we find addiction to be common among NPD sufferers, suggesting only "dual diagnosis treatment" will hold any chances of recovery or improvement. When drugs are involved, often a person with NPD will need to complete a drug detox and treatment regimen all the way through the handling of withdrawal symptoms before anything like NPD is addressed. This can often mean treatment as an in-patient until they move on to subsequent stages of treatment as an out-patient, with a gradual reduction of the drugs they have been addicted, sometimes replaced by less dangerous alternative drugs as therapy, until they are finally in a state where the common treatments for cluster B personality disorders can take place with any kind of results.

ACCOMPANYING DISORDERS

The path to well-being is further complicated by the fact that mental illness often afflicts those it does in clusters, so a person may have several rather than simply one disorder they are dealing with. In fact, there are certain disorders that typically accompany NPD, including:

- Post-traumatic stress disorder (PTSD, over 19 percent)
- Phobia (over 17 percent)
- Bipolar (over 14 percent)
- General anxiety (over 13 percent)
- Depression (over 9 percent)
- Social anxiety (over 8 percent).

When you understand this, it seems clear why we might not alleviate—truly alleviate—the dilemma of an NPD with drugs and alcohol, in fact we've seen that addiction and drug abuse and dependency are *higher* among those with NPD. When you add in the factors above, that their condition is often complicated by other disorders, we find we need to keep them *away* from things like liquor and pot, for example, and that their use of these things whether to self-medicate or as "recreational" activities, only make things worse in both the short and long-term. But the same caveat goes for those with NPD who get dependent and addicted to prescription drugs, as well (Alta Mira).

And by "make things worse," I am no longer talking about how to treat the NPD, but how to protect and make things better for *you,* reading this.

But when we talk about treating the NPD, if we do have a good idea of what got them there—often terrible abuse at the hands of another—we see that it will probably mean getting them through a drug and alcohol ,addiction first, followed by a gradual working through and dealing with the past, including their own deeds, all in a safe and comfortable environment (as possible) for them to do so, until they *break through* all the denial, all the piled-high bricks and blocks they've erected as protective walls around them. Some people have things in the past just too terrible to confront. This often requires a distraction-free setting, if we can get the NPD first to recognize they need the treatment, and then to see they need to devote a great deal to improving (Alta Mira).

A GREAT FIRST STEP

A great, simple, first step, is to get the NPD to simply find and speak with a doctor. If you can reach the person in a non-judgmental way and honesty explain the behavior that concerns you, you might be able to reach them and get them to take action. For that matter, as with any condition, nutrition, exercise, and meditation or prayer can always help improve a person's well-being. Even a person with a cluster B personality disorder might create, maintain, and enjoy healthier relationships if they have personal support and understanding, and ideally treatment. But for our purposes here, and based on my own experiences with my ex-husband and how this started affecting not just me but my kids as well, putting them in actual physical not to mention mental dangers, *leaving* was the first step for all involved.

And of course, if a situation worsens or peaks to where *anyone* is in immediate physical danger to another or to themselves, emergency services should be called upon *immediately* (Burgess).

PART 2:

RECOGNIZING

[6] RECOGNITION

"Nice people don't necessarily fall in love with nice people."

—Jonathan Franzen

NOW THAT YOU have a pretty good idea what the NPD is all about and to some degree why they act the way they do, let's look a little closer at how they behave, or at least, some of the behaviors NPDs seem to hold in common, so you can easily detect them. Again, we are not necessarily out to diagnose Narcissistic Personality Disorder or pretend to be professional therapists. We, more immediately, are interested in simply being *aware* and getting to a place where when we sense narcissistic behavior, whether the person in question is a true-blue NPD or just someone exhibiting the traits, our ears prick up. Awareness is the first step to self-protection, and in protecting others.

With this book, you'll know the clues. Nonetheless I urge you to go well beyond this book. Others have even more information or more authoritative information or might just say things in a different way so it makes more sense to you, because this is, after all, *life and death*. And if not *life and death* in a literal sense, we are still talking about wasted time, wasted energy, wasted potential, and abuse of all forms (and I'll talk about *types* of abuse in this book) which can get so bad as to come close to costing you and yours your very lives, happiness, sanity, and potential. This and other books can supply the knowledge of symptoms, and that's a critical step, but it will be up to you to decide and act upon the clues in your life, *and you have them,* or you might not be reading this book.

But I can help there, as well. When you know someone else has taken action and survived to live happier days, it's encouraging. When you know you need not just an *act* but a *plan,* you're more likely to make and take action on one. And that's what I hope for you.

You *can* chase down symptoms and get to root causes. You can. If you feel great going in to a meeting and not-so-great coming out, you can pause and ask yourself what changed, and very often quickly see, "Oh yes, aha! It was when my mother brought up college in that tone again that I started feeling icky," and you might instantly understand there is a track of arguments you have had with your mother and some of the things she still says and does shows she simply does not seem to understand your choices and so on. You can then act on that or let it go, but the icky feeling should either go away instantly or fade away.

Or, you can go back in your memory and kind of replay the conversation if the answer is not so forthcoming. What I do sometimes is pin-point, "Oh, it was when Kim said what she did about the bar that I like that I felt a little miffed." It will either make sense or you can act or let go as before, but you can usually nail it down. Where there is smoke, there is fire. Fire creates smoke, right?

Read this book. Read others. Have some compassion for yourself. When there's smoke, try to find the source, the fire. If your lover says something off-putting, work it out until it *makes sense.* Armed with the knowledge in this and other books, you will be able to *make sense* out of emotions and behaviors that seem at first to *not* make sense.

And then, you can and should decide, and act.

Here in Part 2, we'll mention or go into depth on 32 traits—or indications or little proofs if you wish— that yes, you are in a relationship with a narcissist. We'll jump start with the nine considered critical for diagnosis by professional therapists, then look at what are likely symptoms *within you* that you are in a relationship with an NPD, obviously we need to look at the traits exhibited by NPDs as well, both *within them* and as actions and tactics they typically utilize. I've been through this, and believe me, it can be eye-opening, scary, surprising, and a big relief as well, all depending, as you go through these aspects of NPD, but in the end, you feel cleaner, freer, and more enabled to confront and tackle your own situation.

[7] JUMP START

"I've had years of psychiatry, and I ask about every six months - it's sort of like getting your oil checked - I ask, 'I'm not an actual narcissist, am I?' The learned men of psychiatry assure me that I meet none of the medical criteria."

—Rob Lowe

LET'S START THE ball rolling with a jump-start, with some quick traits we can learn to look for, because professionals do. For whatever it's worth, it seems more men are narcissists than women (Shouten/Silver), and for professional therapists, NPD is indicated by the presence of five or more of the following factors:

1. Has a grandiose sense of self-importance, demonstrated by exaggerating achievements and talents
2. Is preoccupied by fantasies of unlimited success, brilliance, power, beauty, or ideal love
3. Believes that he or she is "special" and should only associate with other special, high-status people or institutions
4. Requires excessive admiration
5. Has a sense of entitlement, with unrealistic expectations of especially favorable treatment or automatic compliance with his or her expectations
6. Is interpersonally exploitive; takes advantage of others to achieve his or her own ends
7. Lacks empathy; is unwilling to recognize or identify with the feelings and needs of others
8. Is often envious of others
9. Displays an arrogant, haughty attitude[1]

(Shouten/Silver, 69-70)

We would all do well to read and re-read those *nine critical traits above,* as they are what the pros use. From here on out, in Part 2 we'll dive deeper into these and

---

[1] H. Eisenbarth, G. W. Alpers, D. Segre, A. Calogero, and A. Angrilli, "Categorization and Evaluation of Emotional Faces in Psychopathic Women," *Psychiatric Research* 159 (2008), 189-95.

a number of other traits NPDs have been observed and are generally agreed NPDs have/exhibit. Some we will dig pretty deep into, and some we will simply mention (if they are fairly or completely self-explanatory), but all are important, and each has the potential to bring about a true "a-ha!"

I hope you enjoy, and I hope this changes your direction for the better. You are about to see traits and terms used in understanding the NPD, many which will inevitably be familiar as you read them.

[8] SIGNS WITHIN YOU

"People often think that looking in the mirror is about narcissism. Children look at their reflection to see who they are. And they want to see what they can do with it, how plastic they can be, if they can touch their nose with their tongue, or what it looks like when they cross their eyes."

—Anjelica Huston

A STATE OF MAYBE

A CLOSE FRIEND who was in a cult once explained something very telling for me. Almost afraid to ask, I put this to her: "Did you ever have *doubts*?"

"Oh, all the time," she said. I was shocked. She spent twenty years in a cult, "and I *always* had doubts," she said. How could that be? I would have thought she'd either never had any doubts or would have left much sooner. But as I started to understand her history and what happened to her and her cult experience, I started to see similarities and understand my own experience with my NPD even more. Lots of parallels, in fact.

In his book, *Almost a Psychopath: Do I (or Does Someone I Know) Have a Problem with Manipulation and Lack of Empathy?*, (excellent book, by the way) Ronald Shouten, MD, JD, and James Silver , JD describe what they call the "Almost Effect," which is brilliant, and something I have not seen anyplace else. Yet it struck a chord with me right away. I too, like my friend in her cult, spent years in a *maybe* state of mind.

People, maybe you yourself, often have an experience with someone where they feel "That guy bothers, me," and as Shouten and Silver describe, your next words might be, "He's *almost* a psychopath/narcissist/etc."

My friend who was in the cult now looks back and has no doubt she *always* had doubts, fears, could "smell" something not-quite-right, yet she stayed. So did I, in my case, in a toxic, abusive marriage. It was only when things got too dangerous for my kids and this was reinforced by my sister that I finally woke up, smelled the coffee, got out, and when I started looking back, *all the evidence was right there, right in front of my face, all those years.* I either didn't understand the clues or I semi-consciously ignored them. Or I doubted my own gut.

63

Don't doubt your own gut! That doesn't mean you have to believe it wholeheartedly right away without investigation, but I do think if your gut tells you something, you should at least *listen*. I'm aware of a psychic reader whose central message to us is to simply *listen* to our own intuitions. She goes a little further and explains we can also *ask questions* and be open for the answers to arrive. I prayed as a child, gave the practice up, and after my NPD experience, have started meditating and I have tried prayer again as well as simply asking questions of God, the Universe, whatever you prefer, and I have honestly surprised by the answers that seem to arrive. When they do, it usually makes a lot of sense and brings a sense of peace.

And that's the *opposite* of the constant state of *maybe* I used to exist within. In fact, as you are about to see in the following pages, creating a state of personal confusion (a.k.a. "gaslighting") is a natural tactic of the NPD, to put you in a state of confusion.

Recognize it when it happens and know it is a sign that you might be with an NPD.

GETTING SADDER

The longer you are with your NPD the more morose things will become, inevitably. Their pretenses and their façade will inevitably show cracks, and as you get glimpses—which come in odd moments—pay attention to them! They reveal what is going in "inside" your NPD.

ABUSE DENIAL

There is such a thing as "abuse denial." Often, we start to believe that *we* are the abusive ones. This was absolutely the case with me and my ex. Even the guilt, shame, lack of esteem and self-trust, all at the thought that I was somehow the bad one, was there. I guess it was a combination of things that got me to wake up. Even with his starting to abuse my children *right before my eyes,* as all of the people he had us surrounded with, even with our pastor not *telling me* I was in a toxic relationship, it took my sister finally coming to Costa Rica and telling me with concern that "Alex was pretty rough with the kids," that things started to become real. My heart felt like it stopped, because it was all of that reality, which I kind of knew but either couldn't or didn't believe, that was starting to solidify, starting to get real. It was scary, both what it meant about the outside world and what it meant about my inside world—*Was I seeing an alternate reality? And were my kids starting to pay the price?*

I actually felt like *I* was the abusive one, for so long. No longer.

There can of course be other *thoughts, feelings, and behaviors* you seem to carry around that you do not like, and the most important thing is to simply look at them, acknowledge you are having it/them, and then either work out for yourself or with another why these feelings might exist. Sometimes, with heavier experiences or thoughts, it can be best to work them out with someone you trust, and—*spoiler alert*—finding someone to trust and talk to about your situation is going to be one of the first steps you will want to take, if you truly want to improve your life and get free from the negative effects of an NPD.

[9] SIGNS WITHIN THEM

"A Narcissist's Prayer: That didn't happen. And if it did, it wasn't that bad. And if it was, that's not a big deal. And if it is, that's not my fault. And if it was, I didn't mean it. And if I did… You deserved it."

-    reddit.com/r/NarcissisticAbuse/

LACK OF EMPATHY

THE NPD LACKS empathy and can actually seem to either not be aware of or not care that another has needs and desires and thoughts, at all. While the clues NPDs exhibit in plain sight become second nature for the well-read and the trained observer of NPDs (which is what you are becoming, even with this book), I'd have to say the most telling trait, even more than displays of ego, claims of grandiosity, even selfishness, has to be *lack of empathy* (Kluger).

And lack of empathy, as perhaps the classic condition, is more than killing frogs as a kid, as deplorable as that might be. According to Ronald Shouten and James Silver, it's more generally a sign of *psychosis*. As they say:

> "One of the core characteristics of psychopathy, and one that has been studied extensively, is the lack of capacity for empathy (Shouten/Silver, 37)."

> "Psychopathy is a psychological condition in which the individual shows a profound lack of empathy for the feelings of others, a willingness to engage in immoral and antisocial behavior for short-term gains, and extreme egocentricity. Psychopaths do not have the fear response experienced by most of us to the potential negative consequences of criminal or risky behavior and are relatively insensitive to punishment . . . anyone who can feed their need at the moment is potential prey (Shouten/Silver, 18)."

Always Interesting

I now like to think of people in terms of *interested* or *interesting.* If someone is *interested* in you, they ask about you, they think about what you're saying in a conversation—not just what they will say when you're done. They take action to see the good effects on others or the world, not just how it makes them look. If they are *interested* in life, they are extroverted, aware of the wonder "everywhere," and so on.

If someone is compulsively *interesting* they are more *interested in themselves,* more than anything. They do things to look smart and appear strong, amazing, and so on. They are more introverted—even if outgoing, their attention is on themselves. They seem to not genuinely be interested in others at all, perhaps.

It's the simplest, quickest, most reliable measure I know of in deciding if I might be interested in hanging out with a person (pun intended).

Jealous of Attention Given

to Others

Even when another is granted compliments for deeds well-done, the NPD will feel envy at the attention given. This one had a chilling effect on me. As obvious as this trait might seem now as an indication of narcissism, it passed me by with a former "friend." We had a "friend" we'll call Barry, and he gave every "textbook" appearance of being a narcissist, but I was unfamiliar of the significance for a long time. In looking back, there were times he'd go on about how wonderful he was, he only seemed to associate with "important" people, and if you did happen to mention something you were doing or had done that was special in any way, he'd mock it openly, with something like, "Oh, what a big shot!"

ENTITLEMENT

We all feel a little entitlement from time to time, especially after a long week at work, we might feel "entitled" to that paycheck. "Entitlement" has been taken too far in many cases today, according to at least some, who see entitlement as particularly obnoxious, especially when clearly not earned or based on actual accomplishments.

BOASTFULNESS

You can tell a lot about a person by how they speak, as well as by what they do. The NPD sufferer seems to have a constant need to assert his or her own stories and accounts of success or domination, whether real, exaggerated, or imagined.

Sweet & Sour

NPDs aren't abusive 24/7. Sometimes they will be sweet then go back to being abusive. You are being abused none the less. This aspect of a narcissist, in my view, makes it tremendously difficult for them to change. They might *say* they are committed to and will change, but as most victims will agree, they seldom do. Their begs of "please," and promises are meant to buy time, buy compliance, avoid being left or abandoned, and keep you where they want you. To consider change first requires to admit to oneself there is reason to change, and this to an NPD is ridiculous on the surface, as they are clearly superior (it's *you* who must change, after all) and internally, the idea of change is terrifying. It would mean they come face-to-face with their innermost fears of inadequacy—the basis of their disorder in the first place.

Easily Offended

The NPD is ultra-sensitive to criticism. I had a great experience with this one time and it led to the unfolding of a friendship (a fake one). "Barry," used to pride himself on being extremely blunt with people about their misgivings. I decided (before I understood any of this) that I could therefore be blunt with Barry and tell him why he had upset me. He reacted almost violently! It was weird, to say the least.

Taking it Personally

Disagreements with a NPD can often be taken way too personally, or with a bitter sense of humor at best. Remember, they depend on your praise, it's not just a luxury, and when the opposite is handed down but they are not in a situation to reject it honestly, they can take a disingenuous tact or take a simple disagreement too seriously, too personally.,

Doom & Gloom

Despite the constant façade of pride and success, when met with opposition or failure, the NPD will slip into states of gloom and sadness when their insecurities are hinted at or touched upon.

Like a Baby

We all face setbacks and challenges, and we all have ways and means of coping. In fact, they say it's how you respond to just these situations that says so much about who we are and how likely we are to be happy and succeed. The NPD *reacts,* often, as a child might, with outbursts of emotion and dissatisfaction, with petulance.

When we try to understand the root causes of NPD, considering traumas seems at first to make the most sense. As many as 25 percent of all narcissists are believed to be that way thanks to *genetics,* and in all honesty, I could not really see how that could be, unless it were some kind of unlucky, freak chemical combination, but in reading *The Narcissist Next Door,* Jeffrey Kluger draws comparisons with *babies* and their early, all-encompassing and selfish (of course!) behavior. And it clicked—*perhaps the NPD simply has not developed emotionally!*

I recall a business situation where a certain boss was chronically and wholly self-involved, who would rant and actually yell on a fairly regular basis. I, proud of my ability to be terse, described him to a fellow worker as "having the emotional development of an eight-year-old." And alas, in his book, Kluger describes babies as such:

> "Lack of empathy is easily the most important of the disagreeable traits, and in many ways is the hardest for babies to overcome. Not only does the mind of the infant not allow for considering the feelings of others, it doesn't even fully grasp that people or things exist at all once they pass outside the baby's sight or hearing (Kluger)."

It reminds of a kind of horrific moment with the sheriff next door, a classic NPD in my own opinion. The two big giveaways for him in my view were a clear desire to control others and an apparent lack of empathy. I helped him a lot—emotionally through his divorce, with reassurance when his career (in law enforcement) fell apart, and even with occasional tasks around his property. But as soon as I needed a favor or help or anything at all, it was as if there was simply no reason for it, of course. Internally, I decided my family was safer and I was happier *away* from that [expletive]. And life was unpredictable and confusing when we were there, better once we moved.

Add to the above the following traits, and we will have exhausted the traits within the NPD that I have come upon in my research in addition to my own experience with them. These are pretty self-explanatory, and each hold the power to help you connect the dots on the NPDs in your past, present and future. And in the next chapter we'll look at traits that are more action-oriented on the part of an NPD.

Of course, the presence of these or any traits alone do not necessarily an NPD make, but the cumulation, regularity, and severity that do.

In addition to those just discussed, also watch for these in the NPD:

- Over-Inflated Ego
- Exaggerated Self-Importance

- Constant Need for Attention and Flattery
- Materialism and Importance of Wealth and Power

[10] BY THEIR ACTIONS

"Narcissists are people who display a 'toxic selfishness.' They are suffering from the sad reality that the world doesn't actually revolve around them. If you've been dealing with someone who is suspect for narcissistic personality disorder, chances are that you often find yourself feeling 'gaslighted' by their lies, and their cruel, controlling behavior. They will try to convince you that you're imagining things. Or they will blame you – and say you are the true cause of upset. If you try to speak up for yourself, they will come back strong, trying to intimidate you."

———

https://www.notsalmon.com/2018/03/29/quotes-about-narcissists/

LOVE-BOMBING

TOO OFTEN A victim does not realize they are being sucked in until it is too late in many ways. It *is* a kind of brainwashing with victims of NPDs just as with cults. Walk into a cultish group and you'll see what "love-bombing" is, as you are showered with the sincerest of sounding compliments and shown what potential you have to yet to untapped. It doesn't mean those things are not true, but in love-bombing the intention is to draw you in and gain your confidence.

A side note, one of the all-time classic cons involves a five or ten-dollar bill. The con artists drops a bill behind oyu while you are not looking, then taps you on the shoulder before bending down to pick it up and give it "back" to you.

"That's not mine," you say.

"Well, I *know* it's not mine, so it *must* be yours," they say, and they insist you have it.

As they walk off (to be seen again, soon, but not right away) you think, *What an honest person!*

And the next time you meet you are predisposed to believe whatever they say.

Love-bombing gains your affinity and is a classic cult indoctrination tactic, even resorted to time and time again as needed to keep the sheep within the fold. So it is with NPDs, when flattery, apologies, and promises are useful, even if not sincere. Again it doesn't mean you are not smart, good looking, or have great potential, but the intention is suspect, transactional, and what you are dealing for is your devotion, loyalty, and subservience when the time comes. It's dealing with the devil, for sure, or in the least, the Godfather. Strings are attached.

Just as cults love-bomb to draw recruits in, NPDs create a sense of love and warmth to serve their own purposes, and perhaps to also *gaslight* early on in a relationship, so it can be referred and thought back to. "Once a romantic relationship is actually established, there will typically be a golden period. This is the thrilling stage, the dreamy-eyed stage, and it's something narcissists do very well. (Kluger)." In fact, Kluger points out, NPDs are found to be *less likely* to cheat on their partner in the early days but more likely later on as the NPDs sense of entitlement and need for reassurance takes over (Kluger).

As Kluger describes, "The problem is that the honeymoon that follows that courtship doesn't last. The first phase of any relationship with a narcissist is known as the *emergent zone*, and it can be a real, if transient, pleasure . . . It's only in the later phase, what's known as the *enduring zone*, that the egotism, self-absorption and insensitivity of the narcissist emerge (Kluger, 137-138)."

TRIANGULATION

Triangulation is when an NPD creates a milieu of happiness and desirability to draw you in closer.

MIRRORING

Closely related to *love-bombing* and *triangulation* where the NPD uses flattery and a happy environment to lure you in and make you trust them, "mirroring" is when the NPD *seems* to magically like everything you like, be interested in everything you are interested in. It can make you fall in love. It can make you feel like you've fond "the one." You are lulled in to a "safe and trusting space." You let your guard down.

> "There is no reason for you to think this person is anything other than what they've shown themselves to be and you are in love. The sad fact is, that you have fallen in love with yourself, because this person is mirroring you like a parrot. S/he is learning your strengths and weaknesses and all about your insecurities. Mirroring your likes and your dislikes and even agreeing with everything you say is a tactic a narcissist uses to falsely charm you and help them determine what source of supply you will be able to provide them with, sex, money, status, cover, financial. What have your prior relationships been like? What did you tolerate in previous relationships and what can they get away with you? You

are feeding them the script they will have to play with you (Narcissist Abuse Support)."

GASLIGHTING

Gaslighting is another common and classic tactic of narcissists to put you under their dominion. In gaslighting, you are being brainwashed via confusion thrown your way to the point that you doubt your own memory and reality. I recall plenty of arguments with my ex where he would either deny something that occurred or make something up out of whole cloth that I just *knew* was not correct, but by his surprised insistence and reacting like I was crazy, I started to doubt my own reality.

MANIPULATION

These "techniques" are all arrived upon naturally by those who seek to dominate and control. NPDs play mind games, they *have to*. They have undergone some kind of trauma (or perhaps have some genetic defect) that leaves them unable to confront their real situation, and instead believe they must simply *assume or pretend, convince themselves of* a state of superiority to combat and overcome what they do not dare face (even if it no longer exists in present time, even if it's in the past). So they look around for proofs of their dominance, find gratification in manipulating others (Hines).

LIES

NPDs twist the truth, sometimes making things up or omitting them completely. They exaggerate. They create drama. According to Hines, "they will lie about the most basic mundane things simply to gain the most attention, benefit, and fit their own selfish needs and wants."

FORMS AN ENTOURAGE

They surround themselves with what I call an often unwitting "entourage." In fact, I had this realization with my ex-friend who I only became savvy to after a reading by a psychic(!) and started to look at him and the things he did and said with *new eyes*. This was one of many epiphanies I had enunciated for myself *before* I later read about and confirmed what I thought I had observed. I noticed the only people this person could stand to have around were either:

A. Admirers in some way or
B. People "of status" according to the NPD.

I realized I wished to be *neither*. In fact, I redefined for myself what a "friend" really was. In my fish bowl, I had a small pool of people to choose from. Once "out" from under the limitations of the NPD I had something like *7 billion* people on this Earth to choose from. Wow. That perspective creates a real sense of interpersonal abundance, for sure. And ever since, I have not "gone looking for friends," but in the usual course of my days, started to accumulate *very valuable ones*. The truth is, you don't need a million fiends. You need a few good ones. And if you simply get clear on what for you defines a "friend," you'll know them when you see them. For me, this has completely changed my life and happiness.

ASSOCIATES WITH "SUPERIORS"

The NPD, in addition to their own assumptions of *being* superior, seem to seek to validate such an idea with their associations, as well. They often yearn to be associated with those who are famous or rich or superior in some way, and they will let you know about it, too! Name-dropping, spending time with people who would not be their "friends" if not for their wealth or influence (real or imagined) or notoriety…

JUDGEMENT

Intolerance for the flaws (real or imagined) found in others,

APOLOGIES

But never really change, at least not long-term.

BLAME

Everything that happens to you both is of course, somehow, *your* fault.

"YOU'RE OVER-EMOTIONAL"

The reason you have any criticism, of course, when you do, is because you are "over emotional," and you are taking things too personally.

ISOLATION

The NPD is kind of incredible at isolating their victims. They seem to sense who will reveal them and who will not. In my case, my ex did this kind of brilliantly. Even when I was the one who orchestrated our move to Costa Rica, once there, we seemed to always end up with people who would observe our violent, toxic relationship, and despite them, say nothing. I really believe and I know in some cases that he was able to discuss things with them in private before I had any chance to "get to them," and create an impression in other people that I was the one with the mental and emotional issues. I discovered much of this only after we had broken up and separated, that he had said things to them that made them see me as the problem.

I must have played right into his hands with that move—Not only were we geographically isolated, he managed to isolate me socially.

PLAYING THE VICTIM

My ex was the victim in our relationship, according to him, with all of our friends and associates, at least I began to unravel what illusory world he had us nested in.

TRAILS OF DESTRUCTION

They do not care about the harm they do. They *can't*—to care about others would mean they can afford to let go of their desperate façade they believe they must maintain to *live*.

PART 3:
HEALING

[11] FIGURE OUT WHERE YOU ARE

"He that struggles with us strengthens our nerves and sharpens our skill."

—Edmund Burke

FORMS OF ABUSE

WHEN WE TALK about "abuse" at the hands of NPDs, I've found (kind of to my own surprise) that often we dub-in our own experience. For example, when speaking to a group one time after I had left my ex, I discovered during "coffee and cake" time that almost everyone in the room who listened to me speak had their own *form* of abuse at the hands of their NPD. My own was consistently psychological, with occasional physical and yes, sexual abuse at times. For whatever reason, I was in denial and may have even lived with it longer had I not been slapped awake by the abuse starting to reach my *children*. It was a bucket of cold water for me. But after this little talk I gave, one-by-one grateful people approached me and thanked me, related how they appreciated my honesty because they too had suffered one abuse or another. And since—at least for me, part of the healing process has definitely included *understanding*, I think it's helpful to break down the kinds of harm we go through sometimes. I found a handy summation in an article by Hines, listing these kinds of abuse:

- Verbal
- Emotional
- Physical
- Psychological
- Financial
- Sexual
- Spiritual

The good news is when you look at something and start to understand and recognize it, it kind of proofs you to future attacks, and we can better build a new life from these little epiphanies. "If you know you are building a home in a flood zone, you can build one that will withstand floods," as we might say in construction, and in healing, we *are* in construction, in a way.

So, a final step in understanding the NPD in your life (and others) is to understand what has been done to *you*.

HEALING STARTS WITH DIAGNOSIS: DO ANY OF THESE APPLY TO YOU?

Like cults, NPDs seek out people who are demonstrably empathetic, nurturing, or with troubled past or bad fortune. And NPDs find victims in anyone and everyone—no matter race, age, creed, intelligence, ethnicity, wealth or poverty. The only thing all cases have in common is a trail of destruction and confusion. Or more specifically, victims may display symptoms such as:

- Disassociation
- Trauma
- Becoming reclusive
- Anxiety
- Hard time sleeping or eating
- Loss of memory
- Fatigue
- Depression

- Losing "oneself"
- Confusion
- Flashbacks
- Anger
- Hopelessness
- Self-harm
- Loss of interest in life

(Hines)

In scientific terms, victims usually see all of this a little too late and require handling, recovery, and healing. Those actual conditions might include:

- Post-Traumatic Stress Disorder (PTSD)
- Cognitive Dissonance (CD)
- Stockholm Syndrome, where one defends one's captor

YOUR MENTAL STATE

And once you have clear eyes about what has happened and *where you are,* you can start to take steps forward. Yet it's not enough to get to this point and stop, I'm sorry. It's not enough to start to understand the NPD and the narcissists who dabble in some of the traits, nor to learn to detect the traits and those who do them, without taking further steps to improve your situation. Liken it to cancer, because it's an appropriate analogy:

- You felt something was wrong
- You found out what it might be
- By symptoms and ideally, professional input, you diagnosed or decided

And that's where we are! No one in their *right mind* would stop there, at diagnosis. Again, I am not a licensed therapist (yet) and all of this is given simply as my own account *for educational purposes*, and I sincerely hope you will act on positive education and improve your life. If you were to receive a lousy diagnosis such as cancer, I bet you would take actions such as these:

- Find out what can be done
- Find out what has been done successfully
- Find out who can help you
- Start meeting and talking with those who might help you
- Decide on a *plan* and *start*
- Include a team of professionals and put together a support network, knowing there will be challenges ahead
- Monitor your own progress, jockeying along the way to keep things going in the right direction
- Ideally, *arrive at a cure*

- Possibly, help others do the same

It's the path I followed, and here I am, sharing it all in this book so others might also have clarity, hope, and a new life in safety and sanity. Often, this includes for those we love.

YOU ARE NOT A VICTIM

You can no longer afford to be a victim. In fact, I learned that when we *blame* anyone else for our problems, we *make them superior to us.* Think about that. It doesn't mean that nothing was done to you— possibly, *horrible* things have been. What it means is they occurred in part *because you allowed them to.* I am not saying you agreed to any of it, only that the only way forward is with power, and you have some! You have a great deal, actually, but you might not believe that, *yet.* But to start changing your life you will need to acknowledge that perhaps simply by ignorance and by trusting someone, you have been taken advantage of.

Well, you're handling the ignorance part, and in that you have new power. Victim mentality will do nothing but prolong your misery, no matter how "wrong" it might make your NPD.

Today, you are a new, experienced, educated *you,* about to explore your own power. And that's exactly what your NPD has *not* wanted you to do, so we start smartly, and *safely.*

[12] SAFETY & PREPARATION

"When a toxic person can no longer control you, they will try to control how others see you. The misinformation will feel unfair, but stay above it, trusting that other people will eventually see the truth just like you did."

—Jill Blakeway

HELP & INTERVENTION

YOU WILL NOT be doing this alone. Got that? *You will not be doing this alone.* And I mean that even if you are in a situation where you cannot enlist actual people in your presence, you do not have to do this alone. By virtue of finding and reading this book, that in itself means you have found *help,* and you are not alone. But the more help we can muster the safer, the better, the quicker your liberation will be, if things are that extreme. And they can be.

So, first and foremost, if you are in a situation where your safety or the safety of children or anyone else is in jeopardy, before you act make a plan or contact emergency services. Before you flee, have somewhere to flee to. If you will be pursued, have a plan for safety. If you are suicidal, *call someone immediately.* **If appropriate, arrange an intervention or physical assistance with a plan to leave. We are about to talk more about just some of your options in the pages that follow.**

> *If you are alive, you are important, powerful, beautiful, and have a purpose, even if unknown as yet. Believe me, these things unfold as you move forward and it's a very beautiful process!*

Calling the police is fast and simple, but you need to understand the police may have a higher threshold (as they see so much of it) for taking action when a dispute is involved. In other words, they may need to see damage or witness an attack or threats. The police are getting better and better training in recognizing and handling abusive situations, not to mention mental illness.

93

You are a genie about to free yourself from your bottle. **If this wasn't the case, why so much effort to keep you locked up?** You have abilities you have not been allowed to use for a while, and this is precisely what your NPD does not want you to know. Once they do, they will have a hard, hard time getting you back into your bottle. In fact, with all the talk I give about being prepared for a safe and potentially long exodus, I have seen cases where once a person's NPD realizes their victim is now savvy to the fact that they are free, *the NPD* would rather leave than stay! Sometimes they make a lot of noise as they go, but you can actually sense them retreating, to find new, *unwitting* victims. Those who know what's up are too much of a threat, and no longer any fun (Hines).

TO STAY OR GO

Of course, the ideas you are about to read regarding healing apply whether you stay or go. In all likelihood, you will go, but it is possible to stay if the circumstances are right.

So how do you decide if you should stay or go? It's actually pretty simple, if you ask for my *personal opinion*. *There is a 94 percent chance you should leave.* That's the number that leapt to my mind. NPDs are extremely hard to rehabilitate, and you have other concerns for now, anyway, such as your safety and sanity, and those of your loved ones.

My opinion here is based on *toxicity* and your *future*. We can talk about actual, professional diagnosis of NPDs as well as disorders and psychopathy in general, and we can talk about the "almost psychopath," as we have, but where the rubber hits the road in *your life* is what we are doing here, together, in the first place, right? Here are my simple advices, were we holding hands at a coffees shop and getting really real:

- Is your relationship more *toxic* than healthy? Do you often fight or argue in such a way that you never seem to fully heal or to the degree that it affects those around you in a consistently bad way—is it harming the lives of others, too?

- Do you see any hope of the relationship improving *which is based on actual* evidence? Have you been "around this block before," and gotten "back to good?" If this has happened several times or less and it seems very livable, then you might be okay, but you have to be honest about the reoccurrence of battles because the NPD will make things better until things settle down again, as we discuss.

- Is your relationship limiting your life or the lives of others you love?

LET THE WORK BEGIN

You might or might not have decided already if you should stay or go, and either way for now it's okay, we have more to consider, perhaps. The decision starts *internally, with you.* We are starting a *process,* and it's good to bring something like this up and let it "marinade" for a while, so you can start carefully and then proceed confidently. For example, in this age, we are more aware of what's being called *parental narcissism.* It's especially important for children of narcissistic parents to "embrace self-recovery." Once you realize and understand you have a parent who is a narcissist, you like all of us, feel a sense of relief (after any grief, confusion, doubt, and so on) because you realize *it's not you that's crazy.* But the next step is self-recovery, or as it's being called, *internal work* (McBride).

In an excellent article, Karyl McBride Ph.D. explains that such recovery takes three stages:

1. Understanding what has happened, including understanding what a diagnosis of NPD means
2. Dealing with the feelings that exist
3. Looking ahead or reframing your perspective in light of what has occurred and new understandings

According to McBride, the stoic approach of "get over it," won't work in these cases. Neither will simply using mantra-like affirmations or even general psychotherapy. Children of narcissistic parents need *specialized* treatment which includes first handling the trauma involved, and then accepting the *fact* that *your parent is not going to change* (McBride). And *enough is enough*, after a while. So if the change will not likely be with the other party, *the change must begin with you.*

And the hardest part can often be the first part, dealing with the acceptance and grief. It's hard to accept that your father, mother, lover, sister, or someone else close has a limited or no ability for empathy, or that they simply are never likely to truly care about you. The grief comes from the notion of no longer having the father or mother, the lover or friend you *thought* you had, and in the case of narcissistic parents, the grief can come from the shattering of the illusion you thought was your childhood. Even though we know the future will be brighter, it's hard for anyone to let go of what we are used to, what was "normal."

[13] HEALING

"The wound is the place where the Light enters you."

—Rumi

NEW STAGES OF GRIEF

IT CAN HELP to understand the process of healing, and the stages we are likely to go through. When dealing with a break from an NPD who was close to you, the traditionally accepted stages of grief as laid out by Dr. Elisabeth Kubler-Ross in *On Death and Dying* are applicable:

1. Denial
2. Anger
3. Bargaining
4. Depression
5. Acceptance

But in the particular case of a break with an NPD, it's more effective to place our steps in a slightly different order. We have usually already been in a pattern of *denial* and *bargaining* with our NPD, so for us to start recovery, *acceptance* must come first, not last. Only after acceptance can we move on from denial, can we deal with our anger and depression. So in the case of recovering from a relationship with a narcissist, McBride suggests we move through these stages in the following order:

1. **Acceptance**, as we realize the actual problem (the other as NPD)
2. **Denial**, as we deal with our own pattern of denial that our NPD was incapable of true love and caring
3. **Bargaining**, meaning we must re-evaluate the great amount of bargaining we have been engaged in probably on a daily basis both with the NPD (it always seems like we are bargaining!) as well as within ourselves, hoping beyond hope they will change, trying desperately to win their approval
4. **Anger** as we realize just how our needs and best efforts have been wasted, ignored, devalued. The anger can be felt toward both the NPD as well as with ourselves
5. **Depression** as we feel the sadness involved in letting go, even if it's letting go of a "beautiful lie" we have held on to for so long
(McBride)

McBride explains each stage must be fully embraced if we are to move effectively on to the next step of grieving, that each stage laid out above is a kind of prerequisite for moving on to the rest. Expecting guilt, journaling, embracing your feelings and expressing them either in therapy or with loved ones, these things all help you process through your grief and get on with your recovery and your very life. And for recovery, it's not enough to feel sad if you have already felt that way for an extended time (McBride).

These stages are the route out of your grief and out of your internal, damaged, and reduced state as the victim of a NPD, and they are the steps you take to no longer be a victim. It's hard to let go of someone *you love,* and it's hard to accept they have not really loved you. But you must realize that what is now happening, since you have identified you have been falling victim to a NPD, is that this recovery is not about them, but about *you* (McBride).

HEALING IS A PROCESS

Healing is a process that has to be jump-started with an *act*. Liken it to surgery, as the quote at the beginning of the book says:

Truth is like surgery. It hurts but it cures. A lie is like a pain killer. It gives instant relief. But has side effects forever.

—Unknown

To help you jump-start your *road to freedom* I've listed these things you can do to save yourself from the grips of narcissistic manipulation and subjugation. Originally, I had in mind "healing steps," but as pen hit paper I realized there is not necessarily any particular order to these steps (although there can be), and that each person might best follow a different path, and that these are clearly not *all* the possible steps. So, these are tools, and you can and should use the ones that seem best for you and your situation. I'll emphasize when I think a step or tool is indispensable. You need to do what *you* need to do.

I've found that like an injury, "healing" is an appropriate term and healing takes time, evaluation, and for that matter, space. As you start to understand what happened more and more (by evaluation and epiphanies over time, which this books hopes to help accelerate), learn how to detect and prevent it from happening to you ever again (or anyone else, for that matter), and as you put time and space between you and your narcissist, *you do heal.*

[14] THE NEW YOU

"Not until we are lost do we begin to understand ourselves."

—Henry David Thoreau

FINDING YOU, AGAIN

ONE OF THE common things I hear victims of narcissists relate is that they (we) get to a point where we feel *numb* when it comes to *who we are*. "I feel like I completely lost my sense of self in my abusive relationships," says one. "I don't know who or what I am anymore. I have so much fear moving forward and trying to forge a new personality . . . I just feel so lost" (Reddit).

What I can say to that is I've found as a writer (I started writing because I could freelance remotely if I walked a few miles each day into town, away from my NPD), you find your "voice" only by writing, and writing a lot. In so many cases, one has undergone *years* of abuse at the hands of an NPD and it can take just as long to find yourself, truly, once again.

The first step is to make it okay. It's okay to find a hobby, to like and dislike things. Start easy, start with food and music and movies. Start by exploring—take a walk on the beach, in nature, in a city—find what you seem to like.

Do the same with people. When I started understanding what a "friend" really was and recognizing them around me when I met them, it changed my life. I used ot have what I now call "obligatory friends," or people you feel kind of obligated to be friends with because they go to your church or school, and so on. But to me, a *friend* is someone I get excited to see! Someone I have fun with! Someone I laugh with! Someone I can be myself with! Someone who sees positive things in me. There are seven *billion* people in this world and we're now all kind of connected by digital means, so how hard does it seem in that light to find just a handful of good friends? Even one or two? Or a group you like? Sometimes you have to *try* several groups before you find one you feel at home with. So try!

Be honest with yourself about the people you know—do you *like* them? And there is a difference between "like" and "love," of course. You can have one without the other. There are good friends, great friends, and pretend friends. It only took thinking, observing, deciding, and recognizing for me to start a new life with new friends—but only after I had detached from my NPD.

Meanwhile, it's common to experience depression during and even after you leave your NPD. Know that it will diminish as long as you are on the road to more freedom and happiness. It's not a question of how confused or horrible things are around you now, it's about how free and happy they are *where you are headed.*

THE NEW YOU

And you must know that *you will never be the same.* Ask any cancer survivor, any trauma survivor, and they will tell you about the "new normal." Well, "new normal" can be *great.* I'm here to tell you that. I always wanted to be an author, for example, I just never would have guessed this would be the book that started it all!

You do, even if slowly, start to find yourself "re-appear," but it only happens after you get the NPD out of your daily life. I still read what other women go through and many say things like, "It took me five months, but after this long with no contact, I am starting to feel like my old self again, in fact I feel more alive and creative than ever" (Reddit). And that's good news for all of us.

You should not look to form a new personality, but to uncover what and who you really are. That takes time and freedom, and most of all, your own permission. And that, I think, is the start again of personal power. It's a matter of dismantling codependency and simply finding what you *like* again, some of which might be new. People are finding what they like all of their lives, after all. That's part of the joy of living. You have to start small sometimes, or if you have the chance, try big things, but give yourself permission and make the time.

Once I had a small business that was kind of failing, before I was with my ex. I decided I'd be a little schizophrenic about it, because I realized I was working myself to death, and if I were not the only person in the business, if I had any employees, they surely would leave the way I was treating myself. So I started playing two roles. I'd set goals and direction and quotas. I'd then decide something like, "If I sell more than $500 today I'll go have steak for dinner." It was neat because as a manager I would absolutely buy my "employee" a steak if we hit that much in sales, and when I switched and began wearing my salesperson hat, I was excited that there was some kind of reward at the end if I hit what was a realistic goal. And it worked great! In fact I had my best sales that summer, and was able to not only enjoy the work and feel proud and productive, but I saved the down payment and established the credit to buy my first home, and this was all before I met my ex.

So when I came out of the fog, I had a lot to reconnect with, and these lessons served me well. I had lost sight of who I used to be, and gradually realized, "who I used to be," *I still was*. But I'm finding out who I am, even these days, all of four years later, because I am who I was, "plus." I have some serious experiences under my belt, and I've survived it all. It's all scary and exciting at the same time, and I won't make the same mistakes again. With kids, dating is not really Priority A right now, but I imagine there may come a day when it can be.

When you read the testimonials of others who have survived, you see them describe themselves in terms like "more empathy, wiser, more capable than I imagined, more in tune with other people." But maybe my favorite is what ex-cult members say, which is along the lines that while they were "in," they thought they were in the only safe place, that the "outside world" was unsafe and unsavory," but now that they're "out," they clearly see how *limiting* the cult was, and how they feel like they were in a fishbowl, previously. It's a good analogy, especially in terms of the limitations imposed by an NPD (and I would argue that a cult is basically an institutional NPD!).

These ideas helped me leave my old life behind and start a new one, as an *experienced me*. I will never be the same. I have a new normal, but it's a good one. Better, in fact. It's like leaving your childhood behind because we are supposed to grow and become wiser, more independent, and we are supposed to find *new* ways of happiness.

You are now an experienced you. Wisdom does change us. As with children, perhaps some of the magic of youth disappears, but it was based on ignorance, in ways, wasn't it? That doesn't make the memories any less sweet, though, for child or parent. And as we grow and develop we can find new kinds of happiness—in understanding, in sharing, in helping, in giving, and in being strong.

You can, and you will. I believe in you. You found this book, didn't you?

You can learn to love yourself, and you may need to. NPDs rob us of that as much as they can, their domination depends upon it, after all. But we are human beings, full of potential and wonder. Part of overcoming this facet of abuse is the denial. As you leave (and my friend who escaped a cult can attest to this one), you gradually look back and can more accurately assess what happened. It can take years, but it's part of life, and if you believe development is one of the primary reasons for living, maybe people who experience a lot have an unfair advantage in that opportunity to develop!

And you have already begun :)

[15] STAYING

"When I look at narcissism through the vulnerability lens, I see the shame-based fear of being ordinary. I see the fear of never feeling extraordinary enough to be noticed, to be lovable, to belong, or to cultivate a sense of purpose."

—Brené Brown

MY OWN FATHER

STAYING WITH A narcissist *is usually a choice.* And you must know that if you choose to stay you are taking on a certain set of conditions in your relationship. I also understand there are relationships that are hard if not impossible to break off sometimes—parents, children, family members, you name it, and even if you only see one another once a year, understanding them and having a plan for dealing with them can make all the difference in the world.

So, if you are choosing to stay with or stay connected to your narcissist, I will assume there is a good reason and this choice is not simply made out of fear. And I do understand. It's clear to me as I approach the age of 50, that my father, for example, *is a narcissist*. It explains a lot, and he demonstrates *all* if the nine critical traits. He basically has few or no long-term friends, all intimate relationships end in disaster, has always made grand schemes which ultimately fail (which I now understand are more for impressing people and being "special" than for sheer entrepreneurship), and he seems to borrow money eventually from anyone who will agree to it, but when it comes time to pay anyone back, they are suddenly bad people in some way, and he feels no empathy or responsibility for the debt, if he even acknowledges it.

But, when it comes to me and my brother, he has been as good a father as he possibly can. He fought for custody, has been generous *when he has been able,* and clearly loves the both of us very much. The traits do creep in to our relationships at times, but on the whole, he is a different person, it seems, with me and with my brother as well. Further, I am not aware of actual crimes on his part, not violent or sexual or otherwise. If he does have crimes I am unaware of (while many schemes skirt the edge of legality), they would be financial, if I had to guess.

So here is a person with a trail of disaster behind him—personal and financial, and clearly a narcissist, seemingly to everyone but me and my brother. And he is my father, who I talk to about each week and see about each month. I can sustain a relationship, in fact it would cause a great deal more confusion to "disconnect," and I am no longer worried, confused, or suffer a loss of time due to him.

A large, large part of a new sense of tolerance I have for him now is exactly the understandings I am sharing with you in this book.

The "special needs" analogy, I think, is perfect. There are people with dementia, or other disorders or physical ailments who require special handling, and so it seems to be with Dad.

I love my father. He has been as good as he can to me, he has been a great father in so many ways, I enjoy our time together most of the time, and I no longer suffer because of him because I understand him, his condition as a narcissist, and I simply do not agree to things that I might regret, such as getting involved in a business or dropping my own work to help with a new project of his. Even those, I believe he really believes might help me, yet perhaps they are as much to prove his intelligence or superiority, when all others he seems to have been able to get free work out of have moved on.

With my own father, I never quite understood his chronic need to discuss the details of his next big (doomed to fail) venture until the other day, to be honest. It made me sick, but I finally *understood* it, and that made it only slightly more bearable, but completely understandable, and that was a big win, honestly. He was simply and obviously trying to impress the other person at the table with us. It was pathetic, but I finally understood it. I was unable to change the subject and resigned to allow him to explain his new venture. After the meal, I could explain what he was doing to the other party, and my father commented, "Wow, she seemed angry about something, eh?" She did not seem angry at all, but this other party simply didn't get *impressed* by his explanation because she had heard and seen him make extraordinary claims and fail at them before, and they now simply seem ridiculous and boring to her.

Psychology in action. Kind of incredible, actually. But we (she and I) walked away form that without any weird sense of undue influence, any weirdness at all. We could simply laugh it off, unaffected, even if Dad was a little confused, a little frustrated.

Such tolerance is something you will need to be okay with and to get used to. If you are with a narcissist who poses no likely physical threat—and Dad, a narcissist for sure, does not have the traits in the severity that he is a physical threat, only a financial one and a little bit of a psychological one. Think of it like caring for someone with special needs, because that's what they are. Personally, I plan to remain in contact with my father. On the other hand, I cannot imagine an intimate relationship with an NPD, nor a close business relationship, for example.

Six Tips

Living with a narcissist, or any involvement with a narcissist, for that matter, can be extremely frustrating. As we've covered, the early stages of a relationship with a narcissist is usually filled with happiness, even if we now know it to be "mirroring" or "love-bombing." The problem as things progress, the tie becomes both demeaning and demanding. You need to know (and might already) that the relationship will involve your subjugating your desires to theirs and putting up with someone who is both entitled and a know-it-all. These are the realities the relationship will face.

But as with my father, if you have a relationship you'd rather not detach from, Linda Sapadin, Ph.D. both psychologist and success coach offers the following six advices:

1. Determine what behavior your NPD finds non-negotiable. For example, if there is a spending habit that is killing you both and your NPD simply won't stop. If you can let it slide, so be it.

2. Recognize *gaslighting*. NPDs say things they later deny or alter. It's weird. It's meant to throw you off and make you feel confused and stupid, to keep you under control. Be alert to it if this is one of your NPDs traits, and if you choose to stay, it would help to know how you will accept or handle such a tactic in advance.

3. Insist on respect. With my NPD, the fights kept getting worse, kept getting more physical. I *had to* decide on limits and how to end or stall an argument initially for the sake of the kids. As your relationship goes on, it's likely the fights and the demeaning outbursts will get worse, so be prepared to walk away or insist on apologies when they do.

4. Learn to negotiate. Find where your power and leverage are and when you need to use them, especially on the important issues. Developing better negotiating skills will be of terrific value.

5. Steele your self-esteem. You are in for an all-out assault on your self-worth, so be preparing in advance to deal with it. This can mean regular visits to the gym and staying healthy for a better self-image, meditating, affirmations, and friends and family who are supportive and reaffirm your value. Your inner-talk makes a *huge* difference as well, which we often neglect.

6. Don't lie or cover up what is happening to you. Many NPD victims are embarrassed or confused about their relationship and will gloss over such things when discussing with friends or go so far as to deny observations made by others. You will want *someone* to be open and honest with outside of yourself about the narcissist and your relationship, whether it's Dad, Mom, your child, spouse, lover, or co-worker.

(Sapadin)

Narcissists are *hard to change* and most would agree changing people short of therapy or major life events can seem impossible, so know what you're up against and plan for it. Dr. Sapadin's six guidelines will go a long way, and possibly preserve a relationship if you want to.

ADMIT YOUR OWN NEED

In many a 12-step program, the very first step is to deal with *powerlessness*. And the good news is that it can be—paradoxically—*empowering* to admit your own powerlessness. Think of it this way, as an extreme example (drawing upon extremes can be a fantastic way to illuminate things): Let's say you have to change a tire on your car. Without thinking you'd probably first go find a jack to lift the car with. Well, you have in a way admitted a powerlessness, have you not? And all it meant was you needed a tool or some help, or something else.

When you see that you have been victim to an NPD and decide *ENOUGH IS ENOUGH,* it would be crazy to expect different results without change, right? Let's take this a little step further. In *You Need Help! A Step-by-Step Plan to Convince a Loved One to Get Counseling* by Mark S. Komrad, MD (excellent book, by the way, and an easy read), he suggests the following message be communicated to the person you wish to help. In our case, that person is *you:*

"… this situation is beyond me, and we need someone who is used to sorting out these kinds of problems and can give some suggestions about how to help" (Komrad, 126).

So, you might piece together something of a mastermind or team of allies for enduring your life with an NPD or narcissist, or to make it across your runway, if you can't leave right away but plan to. Regardless of what you ultimately do, you should not go it alone. In fact, "alone" is the ally of the narcissist, as they like to isolate you, both physically and mentally, as well as socially and even with family.

Consider the following as potential "team members":

- Your family physician
- A sibling or friend
- Clergy
- A support group
- And even people you discover through books and media (however I am writing under a pseudonym)

If I were advising someone to help *you,* I would first tell them to simply let you *speak,* to listen to you without interrupting, and to not judge. I'd tell them to *believe* you and not try to justify or reason away the things you might be saying. And I would be very sure they didn't in any way *blame* you for these things that you tell them have taken place. They should simply listen and be supportive, and to do this *genuinely*. People can sniff out when they are being patronized.

I would tell them to give you support, validation, approval, acceptance, love, and acknowledgement. I would also make sure they understand that in a relationship with an NPD you have been subject to mind games, trickery, and very likely abuse you might not even yet disclose. I'd tell them that you have been subject to domination, intimidation, and likely depression and isolation as well. I would tell the this all results in self-doubt, loss of self, low self-esteem, and confusion on the most basic of things like "who you are," and "whose fault this all is."

And I would tell them to *never* suggest you should "just get over it!"

What I would tell them is that what you really need is a *friend,* a person who will listen without judgement, be supportive, and provide a safe space for you to relate all of these things just as you wish and need to, and that letting you *speak* is the first and very important step in reversing the situation you have been in.

To you, I say to get things changing, to start your healing, you need to find such a person, and simply start by *speaking.*

Also consider therapy. Komrad says, "When someone you care about is in obvious emotional pain, giving a nudge toward a professional assessment or treatment is not meddling, it is *caring*. It is an expression of compassion. It is consistent with religious traditions to 'Love thy neighbor as thyself' (Komrad, 25)."

So my advice to you, as the victim here, is "Love yourself as you'd love your neighbor." To see someone suffering and not do anything, that is a crime, it's something that many of us do, but then find it hard to live with and thus resolve to make sure we do go out of our way to see the woman down the street is not beat anymore, nor the child, so why not *you*? And with *you*, the task is all the easier. But back to Komrad's advice, *seek professional assessment or treatment*. It's easier than ever. Heck, it's possible by video conference, now.

GIVE YOURSELF A BREAK

Becoming a victim of an NPD can happen to *anyone*. As a friend who left a cult likes to say, "There are still lots of smarter, more successful people than me in there!" So don't be so quick to assume it's a matter of *intelligence*, per say, even if the experience makes you feel kind of stupid. In fact, in that particular cult, she tells me she believes there are a few types of people who seem attracted to it:

- Egomaniacs who want to be like gods;

- Very, very good people who see in it a way to better the world, despite whatever sacrifices they have to make, personally;
- "Gullibles."

And she tells me she feels she was maybe a little bit of each.

I don't think this is exactly the same for victims of NPDs, but I think it's interesting enough and illuminating enough to mention here. And, it says to us all, "Give yourself a break!" Sometimes being a victim, being gullible, being *had,* says something positive about you, if naïve. And as you recover, guess what seems to happen? Your naivete gets replaced by wisdom and cynicism, and we can gradually remove the latter over time as you heal. Even if keeping a little bit is healthy.

Hindsight *is* 20/20 but do you know there's actually a term for this? It's *retrospectoscope* (Shouten/Silver, 88). We all feel a little stupid sometimes, when something happens we wish we had prevented, especially after we have been taken advantage of, particularly sexually and so on. Believe me, I know. And I have *uber-empathy* for those who experience the shame of being had in any way. It makes me want to dish out justice, myself. It's part of why I wrote this book. But I've learned a few things, too.

1. Good people don't expect people to be bad. It makes us vulnerable, at least for a while.

There's a healthy balance between naivete and cynicism.

2. The *retrospectoscope* is *fictional*. It's an imaginary instrument that allows us to look back in time and predict future events, but the future cannot be completely predicted, *that's why it's called the future!*

3. Love is blind—especially at first and usually for a limited time. It's further muddled by the existence of *infatuation* and *wanderlust*. These things can make you think you're in love when, if you work out what your own criteria for being "in love" are, (just as you should what a true "friend" is), you'll see infatuation and wanderlust can seem a lot like love, and not always be or lead to love.

MOST OF ALL, if you are with an NPD, keep in mind you deserve compassion, which they are not likely all the time to give, so you *must* insist upon it. And if you are not getting basic human needs from your NPD but choose or cannot disconnect, at least compensate and seek human compassion to make up for it in other places. It just means you must steel yourself by finding and keeping good friends, and helpful allies.

"The value of compassion cannot be over-emphasized . . . No greater burden can be borne by an individual than to know no one cares or understands."

—Arthur H. Stainback

[16] LEAVING (OPTIONAL BUT LIKELY)

"Freedom is never voluntarily given by the oppressor; it must be demanded by the oppressed."

—Martin Luther King, Jr.

THE ELEPHANT ROPE

LOOK, LEAVING CAN be hard. Not just because of the emotional uncertainty, but in terms of safety and money. This is so true that there are groups created to *help you leave*. And in looking back, I feel like I was that elephant in the story about the rope. When there were circuses, and an elephant was a baby, they would leash him or her with a rope. As the elephant grew, of course, it would gain in size to where that little rope could be easily snapped with a little effort—*but the elephant doesn't know that.* So, "elephant rope" has been an analogy used in self-improvement to symbolize anything—any system or imagined penalty or just a belief that one cannot leave or break free. In looking back, I'm amazed at how, given the way things eventually did work out for me to leave my ex, it could have been so simple to leave at any earlier time. Ultimately, as I've described, I was left with four small children in a foreign country with almost no money at all.

Cults sometimes take your passport and threaten that if you doubt the group or heaven forbid, leave, you will be cut off from all friends and family, all resources to survive with, and they often follow through on those threats. So a first sign of being caged is when an NPD or anyone for that matter starts to try to limit your thoughts, limit your exposure to information, limit you in all kinds of ways. So it can be kind of amazing to look back and realize, *I could have just walked away at any time.* That's not always the case, of course, like where kids are involved, or if you have no identification, no money, and so on.

SAFE ESCAPE

On Reddit, a fellow named Chris explains, "*Operation: Safe Escape* initiative is our program to combat domestic violence and help people safely escape an abusive situation. We work with both victims of domestic violence and shelters/safe houses to improve the security of both. As a non-profit, this is something we do for free." Chris is a security specialist who works and teaches security for the federal government. They have designed a phone app based on the "escape plan" used by many domestic violence shelters but they have taken the app from paper form and put in on your phone, disguised as a "Quote of the Day" password-protected app, in case your NPD gets a hold of your phone. There really are inspirational "quotes of the day," but there's also a password-protected area to assist you in leaving safely, which can take time and planning, and most of all, *help*.

The app for Apple phones can be found here:

https://apps.apple.com/us/app/quote-mania/id1225342669

The real point is to have a plan and to know that there are resources, many of them. Access to the internet alone can provide a wealth of resources, and many are named in this book for you.

I had a friend, call her Danni, who was young, ambitious, intelligent, and beautiful. I was her manager at the real estate office where she was a top-producing agent. She sat through a meeting one day in sunglasses, which I briefly noted as odd, and she asked to see me outside when it was over. After wrapping up quickly with another, I went outside to see what was up. Before she removed her glasses I realized she was covered in bruises.

"What happened?" I asked and before she got her glasses off she broke down and I understood—she had been *beaten*. A rush of reality and urgency overcame me, and I just wanted to comfort and reassure her, to help her however I could. By my insistence, we made immediate arrangements. I would park near her husband's business and watch his car as she got the things she needed from their home and *left*. Over the coming weeks I would play intermediary as they negotiated the breakup.

But we both knew she could not ever go back to him.

I believe physical abuse is akin to psychological abuse in that they both stem from deep-seated instincts in another. And no matter how much we analyze and understand and try to heal those afflicted, when the potential for damage to another is always there as a possibility, there is really one choice.

Leave.

Leave in the safest possible way but *leave*. Put time, space, your own power and possibly the power of the state between you. You are not here to devote your life, your safety, your happiness, to another, necessarily. In fact the good you can do in this life unhampered I believe far outweighs devotion to any one individual, especially when that other is afflicted with pathology.

One day, we may have the know-how to change a bull into a cow, but until then, I say it is far too risky to "help a bull out of a ditch," especially when it's *you* they might kill for the effort, and especially all on your own.

And stop looking for happiness
in the same place you lost it.

[17] LOOKING AHEAD

"Happiness is not something you postpone for the future; it is something you design for the present."

—Jim Rohn

INDEPENDENCE

AS I WATCHED a good friend once completely deteriorate and lose herself over her divorce, what struck me most was how profoundly dependent she was on her soon-to-be ex-husband *economically*. I was trying to understand her despair and her absolute desperation at the idea of losing who, for all outside observers, was *not a good husband in the first place*. To try to make sense of it in any way, I concluded one of the major components was in fact economics. It could be argued that this was part of her fear, whether she knew it or not. Another part was emotional dependence, of course, but the economics thing really struck me. It sounds base, it sounds a little ugly, but it's true.

We do need basic needs met like food and shelter and it seemed to me that my friend was sensing on some level that without her ex she might not be able to support herself, which might have led, in her mind, to all sorts of imagined horrors, including a loss of safety, integrity, friends, the respect of her daughter (which she started to lose anyway in her desperate acts during the divorce), maybe even loss of food and shelter.

I realized how important economics, for one thing, is to being able to sustain one's own integrity. *How many battered wives never leave because they don't see how they can make it financially and in other ways without the abusive partner supporting them?* After all, how often is that the case, that the abuser is also the one the victim depends upon. I *thought* I was dependent on my own ex, until he actually abandoned us and I had to make it on my own anyway. It's only now, after he's gone that I realize how much *I supported him.* So one of the things I teach my children is that it's important to be independent, in some nany ways, but particularly economically.

NPDs seem to understand this and therefore discourage their victims from improving their lives, either for fear of the victim no longer needing them or for fear of their victim meeting new people to expose their arrangement to, and so on.

So one of the steps in healing is very definitely seeking and creating new independence. It might involve taking night classes and finishing that degree or learning a new, exchangeable skill. You might have to become *dependent* for a limited while until you can fly on your own, which I see a lot of former victims avoid. It's hard to leave an abusive relationship and jump right into a situation where you are now dependent on friends and family for a while, *but we all go through something like this.*

As part of your healing, you will absolutely need to rely on and get help from others for a while—It's actually a big part of the healing process I prescribe—do not go this alone. You have been going it alone and it has not worked out that well, right? It doesn't mean you are not and will now be independent, but unless you already have a law degree or real estate license you can simply dust off and get back into the game, in your big picture, doesn't it make sense to make an arrangement—a temporary arrangement at least—that will result in the independence you need to provide good, new lives for you and your kids, for example?

I had an uncle who was basically outcast form the family because he and his wife and kids lived very simply while he dragged them all through his finishing law school, *but now he's a lawyer, loves what he does, and the rest of the family looks to him when they need financial help or advice.* So see your big picture.

FOCUS ON HEALING

Anger *is* an appropriate emotion to feel, an appropriate response when one has been abused, but revenge and prolonged obsession with it or any abuser can be self-defeating. It can prolong or delay healing, it can put off your future even further. There is justice, and there is forgiveness, and these are a bit outside the purview of this short book. What this book and what I am wholly concerned with as far as you are concerned is your immediate safety and your sanity. You should always row safely across the river *before* throwing stones at the alligators.

This is an opportunity to create a new, bigger picture, for you and your family. You need to make sure your *healing* is progressing, even while protecting yourself. It's not enough to do one of those exclusively.

You will be dealing with grief and sadness, for sure, it's always hard to make major life changes and to say goodbye to someone, but I can tell you, when you do get free from the NPD who has been keeping you down, there is freedom like you have not tasted in a long time, perhaps never before.

I see so many today deal with their grief and sadness by *dwelling* on it, and while I do strongly encourage therapy in this book, there is nothing like getting busy on proactive, positive actions to take charge of your life. It's what worked for me, and it still works for me.

Finally, in looking ahead, understand you will need to give yourself time. Any capable manager can tell you it can take a year or more to rebound from a financial emergency or to rebuild your personal credit, so why expect to be completely happy and healthy in less than that? It takes whatever it takes, but if you find and head "north," you *will* make it there. All the faster with constant learning, evaluating, and making positive decisions and actions that keep you on your *new path*.

CONCLUSION

"I was a solipsist and a narcissist and much too arrogant. I have a lot more compassion now, but it took a long time."

—Andrew Sarris

TODAY, I UNDERSTAND there are people who have experienced some crushing trauma to their self-esteem and rebounded by over-compensating with self-importance and become what we call *narcissists*. It makes all kinds of sense to me now. I have seen it in the extreme with people who I believe were sexually, physically, or mentally abused as children, and gone on to decide they are more important than others, and if I had to guess, *more important than what happened to them.*

It's going on four years since my situation reached what was the limit for me, I saw what it was doing, finally, to me, and I saw what it was beginning to do to my kids. My ex, who was physically beaten regularly as a child himself, was starting to beat our children.

Maybe I was lucky, because *he left us in Costa Rica,* making the "leave" option easy enough, if one of the scariest things I've ever experienced. But I realize for anyone codependent and in a situation they try to see through rose-colored glasses, it must be *seem* impossible to leave. After all, you *think* you're in love, right? You *think* you are wholly dependent on this other person—after all, that's exactly what they have worked to make you feel and believe all this time, and you might also be economically dependent on the other, on the NPD, which is what they also want you to believe.

In my case, while it sounds very dramatic—*and it was!*—my ex leaving us high and dry in a foreign country after he emptied the bank account and flew back to the U.S., might have actually been a strange blessing, after all. Necessity is *a mother,* that's for sure, but here we are. While I still have legal fees and an occasional ally of my NPD ex to contend with on Facebook, my kids are no longer in danger, I am no longer in danger, and I have had the freedom to *explore healing* for about four years now. It's *still* a process.

They say you can estimate the time it takes to get over something, like "a week for every month you were together," or more generally, "eleven weeks" to develop strong coping strategies after a breakup, or "half the time you were together," or in the case of a sudden loss of a loved one, "never"—you just gradually conform to a "new normal" (Levine). What that says to me is *it can take a long, long time.* But you do grow. And I have been doing better and better.

In fact, I took my own advice. It's what you find in this book. I allowed myself time for introspection and permitted myself time to heal. As time has gone by and thoughts have bubbled to surface and fly away, I feel like I have understood more and more. Part of why I wrote this book was for my own healing, and that work in large degree because you *really* learn something once you try to teach it. And we learn in different ways, one of those being "hearing yourself say it."

And after all this time and care I've allowed myself, I might have made my biggest breakthrough of all just recently, in the act of writing this book, to tell you the truth. See, as you learn the traits and causes of a narcissist for yourself, and as you look back and look around to confirm these things for yourself, it starts to make some kind of sense. You detach more and more. In fact, something internal and kind of magic can start to happen. For me, I started to see some of the behaviors in my own life and tweak them. I'm not so judgmental of my kids. I don't take criticism so personally. I don't care about being the center of attention. And it's been easy. I see those things now. Whether I had any inclination to do some of these things myself in any degree because of genetics or upbringing or the influence of the NPDs in my life or just because "it's normal," none of that really matters.

I am *cause* over these things because I am aware of them. It feels great. And in finding one of my new friends—who is *beautiful,* by the way—had any self-doubts, I was kind of shocked and concerned. How unjust! How silly! I became very sensitive to their needs and I wanted her to "see herself through my eyes," and I told her so.

And after a few days of this, I felt a kind of beauty. And I'm sorry, I can't describe it any better than that, even though I claim now to be a writer. But it did occur to me, now that I feel so free to care so much about another, *maybe I am on the road to healing.*

Pretty neat, right?

Sometimes I still worry that I haven't done well enough for my kids. Sometimes I'm ashamed we don't have more, that I dragged them through what we all went through, that I haven't given my kids the American Dream—that pretty little house with the white picket fence and a dog in the yard. I even realize it was *my kids* who saved *me,* who got me to see the light and leave an abusive situation, and I'm so grateful and humbled. Then, looking at them as they go about their days, I remember my own advice to myself, the one about giving yourself a break, and I realize maybe I did—maybe I *am* giving them the American Dream, the version where our kids do better than we did.

My parents, I believe, were each abused, and each show some degree of severity of NPD as a result. While neither is criminal, both have made decent successes of themselves, both have even been good grandparents, I do see how what small degree of NPD symptoms they each exhibit have limited them in various ways. At the same time, while they might have each been abused, neither abused *me.*

I, in turn, have never laid a violent hand on my own kids. And any tendency to drop into NPD behaviors, while mild on my part, has been largely arrested by my own advance in knowledge and thinking on the matter, even if my own parent were completely ignorant to it. Further, I have managed to get my kids out of an abusive and toxic family situation.

And the future is now wide open, and I am stronger. I am now more capable of providing what really matters—a loving heart, understanding, and a view that we each are here to experience and learn, to support each other and develop, and to leave things a little better than we found them.

So, in that, I feel like a glowing success, and I start to love myself again.

—Christine Murray

THANK YOU

THANK YOU for taking the time to read my book. If you found this information useful in any way, I would greatly appreciate feedback.

If you can, leave a review. Leaving a review allows me to see where I can improve and increases the chances other people will see this book, which will possibly help them as well.

ABOUT THE AUTHOR

CHRISTINE MURRAY (pseudonym) was born in New York, raised in Florida, and whisked away to Costa Rica where her husband arguably with Narcissistic Personality Disorder managed to isolate and subjugate her, possibly for the rest of her life and despite their small circle of friends and church, until she saw what their toxic relationship was doing to their *kids*.

With family a thousand miles away, no helpful friends, and no money, she reinvented herself as a writer, walking miles each day to use the community Wi-Fi and freelance at a penny-per-word until through her hard work she saved enough to move and through diligent research, she started to understand her dilemma.

Today, she is a therapist in training and writer with her four children and two dogs, living happily together in Ventura, California.

RESOURCES

REDDIT

FOR THIS BOOK, I relied on both my own experiences as well as an incredible, online resource:

https://www.reddit.com/r/NarcissisticAbuse/

The above is a segment or area of Reddit, called a "subreddit," that has over 34,000 members who discuss their own experiences and what worked for them. There are also segments that deal specifically with narcissistic parents and spouses. Check it out! Join! Discuss! Get free! Finding out you're not alone can be the first, most powerful step. Feeling like you're helping others by sharing can be just as powerful a part of your healing (it's why I wrote this book!).

According to the Reddit page, it was created as "a place for targets of a narcissist's abuse to come together to support, encourage, learn from, share with, and validate one another."

This Reddit page is full of valuable resources, even alternatives of one cannot afford therapy. There are also "subreddits" that deal specifically with narcissists and divorce, narcissistic parents, and so on.

ALTA MIRA

ALTA MIRA is "a premier residential treatment center specializing in alcohol and drug addiction, and complex co-occurring disorders."

Get help by calling them to find out more:

1 (866) 234-0492

And please see the WORKS CITED section that follows. I recommend all of the sources listed there.

INSPIRATION

"Just like there's always time for pain, there's always time for healing."

—Jennifer Brown

"It's a deep and all but certain truth about narcissistic personalities that to meet them is to love them, but to know them well is to find them unbearable. Confidence quickly curdles into arrogance; smarts turn to smugness; charm turns to smarm."

—Jeffrey Kluger

"Better to die fighting for freedom than be a prisoner all the days of your life."

—Bob Marley

"For to be free is not merely to cast off one's chains, but to live in a way that respects and enhances the freedom of others."

—Nelson Mandela

"Freedom lies in being bold."

—Robert Frost

"None but ourselves can free our minds."

—Bob Marley

"Between stimulus and response there is a space. In that space is our power to choose our response. In our response lies our growth and our freedom."

—Viktor Frankl

"Love is what we are born with. Fear is what we learn. The spiritual journey is the unlearning of fear and prejudices and the acceptance of love back in our hearts. Love is the essential reality and our purpose on earth. To be consciously aware of it, to experience love in ourselves and others, is the meaning of life. Meaning does not lie in things. Meaning lies in us."

—Marianne Williamson

"A friend is someone who gives you total freedom to be yourself."

—Jim Morrison

"Freedom is not worth having if it does not include the freedom to make mistakes."

—Mahatma Gandhi

"Then only journey is the journey within."

—Rainer Maria Rilke

"Rock bottom became the solid foundation on which I rebuilt my life."

—J.K. Rowling

"Believe in yourself and all that you are. Know that there is something inside you that is greater than any obstacle."

—Christian D. Larson

"If you are distressed by anything external, the pain is not due to the thing itself, but to your estimate of it; and this you have the power to revoke at any moment."

—Marcus Aurelius

"Promise me you'll always remember: You're braver than you believe, and stronger than you seem, and smarter than you think."

—A.A. Milne

"The past cannot be changed. The future is yet in your power."

—Unknown

"Learn to enjoy every minute of your life. Be happy now. Don't wait for something outside of yourself to make you happy in the future. Think how really precious is the time you have to spend, whether it's at work or with your family. Every minute should be enjoyed and savored."

—Earl Nightingale

"Infuse your life with action. Don't wait for it to happen. Make it happen. Make your own future. Make your own hope. Make your own love. And whatever your beliefs, honor your creator, not by passively waiting for grace to come down from upon high, but by doing what you can to make grace happen... yourself, right now, right down here on Earth."

—Bradley Whitford

"For me, singing sad songs often has a way of healing a situation. It gets the hurt out in the open into the light, out of the darkness."

—Reba McEntire

"Music has healing power. It has the ability to take people out of themselves for a few hours."

—Elton John

"It's always hard to deal with injuries mentally, but I like to think about it as a new beginning. I can't change what happened, so the focus needs to go toward healing and coming back stronger than before."

—Carli Lloyd

"I wish that people would stop destroying other people just because they were once destroyed."

—Karen Salmansohn

"The friend who can be silent with us in a moment of despair or confusion, who can stay with us in an hour of grief and bereavement, who can tolerate not knowing... not healing, not curing... that is a friend who cares."

—Henri Nouwen

"I actually think sadness and darkness can be very beautiful and healing."

—Duncan Sheik

"The greatest healing therapy is friendship and love."

—Hubert H. Humphrey

"Healing is a matter of time, but it is sometimes also a matter of opportunity."

—Hippocrates

"Part of the healing process is sharing with other people who care."

—Jerry Cantrell

"I have a huge belief in the importance of bees, not just for their honey, which is a healing and delicious food, but the necessity of bee colonies that are vital to the health of the planet."

—Trudie Styler

"The wilderness is healing, a therapy for the soul."

—Nicholas Kristof

"Healing takes courage, and we all have courage, even if we have to dig a little to find it."

—Tori Amos

"Kindness and a generous spirit go a long way. And a sense of humor. It's like medicine - very healing."

—Max Irons

"Time begins the healing process of wounds cut deeply by oppression. We soothe ourselves with the salve of attempted indifference, accepting the false pattern set up by the horrible restriction of Jim Crow laws."

—Rosa Parks

"Ten years ago, I still feared loss enough to abandon myself in order to keep things stable. I'd smile when I was sad, pretend to like people who appalled me. What I now know is that losses aren't cataclysmic if they teach the heart and soul their natural cycle of breaking and healing."

—Martha Beck

"The art of healing comes from nature, not from the physician. Therefore the physician must start from nature, with an open mind."

—Paracelsus

"What happens when people open their hearts?"

"They get better."

—Haruki Murakami

"I'm here. I love you. I don't care if you need to stay up crying all night long, I will stay with you. If you need the medication again, go ahead and take it—I will love you through that, as well. If you don't need the medication, I will love you, too. There's nothing you can ever do to lose my love. I will protect you until you die, and after your death I will still protect you. I am stronger than

Depression and I am braver than
Loneliness and nothing will ever
exhaust me."

—Elizabeth Gilbert

"It has been said, 'time heals all
wounds.' I do not agree. The wounds
remain. In time, the mind, protecting
its sanity, covers them with scar tissue
and the pain lessens. But it is never
gone."

—Rose Fitzgerald Kennedy

"The emotion that can break your
heart is sometimes the very one that
heals it..."

—Nicholas Sparks

"Scars have the strange power to
remind us that our past is real."

— Cormac McCarthy

"Pain is a pesky part of being human,
I've learned it feels like a stab wound

to the heart, something I wish we could all do without, in our lives here. Pain is a sudden hurt that can't be escaped. But then I have also learned that because of pain, I can feel the beauty, tenderness, and freedom of healing. Pain feels like a fast stab wound to the heart. But then healing feels like the wind against your face when you are spreading your wings and flying through the air! We may not have wings growing out of our backs, but healing is the closest thing that will give us that wind against our faces."

—C. JoyBell

"The soul is healed by being with children."

—Fyodor Dostoevsky

"Hearts are breakable," Isabelle said. "And I think even when you heal, you're never what you were before."

—Cassandra Clare

"Our wounds are often the openings into the best and most beautiful part of us."

—David Richo

"Poetry heals the wounds inflicted by reason."

—Novalis

"Change, like healing, takes time."

—Veronica Roth

"As my sufferings mounted I soon realized that there were two ways in which I could respond to my situation -- either to react with bitterness or seek to transform the suffering into a creative force. I decided to follow the latter course."

—Martin Luther King Jr.

"To be rejected by someone doesn't mean you should also reject yourself or that you should think of yourself as a lesser person. It doesn't mean that nobody will ever love you anymore. Remember that only ONE person has rejected you at the moment, and it

only hurt so much because to you,
that person's opinion symbolized the
opinion of the whole world, of God."

—Jocelyn Soriano

"do not look for healing
at the feet of those
who broke you"

—Rupi Kaur

"The best relationships in our lives are
the best not because they have been
the happiest ones, they are that way
because they have stayed strong
through the most tormentful of
storms."

—Pandora Poikilos

"Yes, I understand why things had to
happen this way. I understand his
reason for causing me pain. But mere
understanding does not chase away
the hurt. It does not call upon the sun
when dark clouds have loomed over
me. Let the rain come then if it must

come! And let it wash away the dust
that hurt my eyes!"

—Jocelyn Soriano

WORKS CITED

I'VE FOUND VALUABLE insights in the following
web sites and books. I recommend all of them:

WEB SITES

Listed Alphabetically

Alta Mira Recovery Programs. "Narcissistic
     Personality Disorder and Addiction Treatment."
     (Accessed 2019-08-20). Retrieved from
     https://www.altamirarecovery.com/co-occurring-
     disorders/addiction-and-narcissistic-personality-
     disorder/

Burgess, Lana. (reviewed 2018, January 4 by Timothy J. Legg, PhD, CRNP). "What are cluster B personality disorders?" Retrieved from https://www.medicalnewstoday.com/articles/320508.php

Hines, Donna. (2014, October 30). "Narcissistic Victim Syndrome and How to Help Victims Heal." Retrieved from https://www.linkedin.com/pulse/20141030165049-141613845-narcissistic-victim-syndrome-and-how-to-help-victims-heal/

Levine, Sarah. (2015, January 20). "How Long Does It Take To Get Over A Breakup? Science Says Three Months, So Keep Your Head Up." Retrieved from https://www.bustle.com/articles/59646-how-long-does-it-take-to-get-over-a-breakup-science-says-three-months-so-keep

McBride Ph.D., Karyl. (2012, May 7). "It's All About Me! Recovery for Adult Children of Narcissist: Internal work is crucial for ultimate peace of mind." Retrieved from https://www.psychologytoday.com/us/blog/the-legacy-distorted-love/201205/it-s-all-about-me-recovery-adult-children-narcissist

Mental Health America. (Accessed 2019, August 30). "Co-Dependency." Retrieved from https://www.mentalhealthamerica.net/co-dependency

Narcissist Abuse Support. (Accessed 2019, September 3). "Mirroring." Retrieved from https://narcissistabusesupport.com/red-flags/narcissist-red-flag-mirroring/

Personal Growth. (2018, May 6). "Here's How Reassuring You Can Be, Based on Your Personality Type." Retrieved from https://personalitygrowth.com/heres-how-reassuring-you-can-be-based-on-your-personality-type/

Reddit (website, accessed 2019, August 1-22). Retrieved from https://www.reddit.com/r/NarcissisticAbuse/

Sapadin, Ph.D., Linda. (Updated 2018, July 8). "How to Live with a Narcissist." Retrieved from https://psychcentral.com/blog/how-to-live-with-a-narcissist/

Scott MS, Elizabeth. (updated 2019, July 22). "How to Identify a Malignant Narcissist." Retrieved from https://www.verywellmind.com/how-to-recognize-a-narcissist-4164528

BOOKS

Listed Alphabetically

Capps, Donald. *Understanding Psychosis: Issues and Challenges for Sufferers, Families, and Friends.* Rowman & Littlefield Publishers, Inc., 2010.

Kluger, Jeffrey. *The Narcissist Next Door: Understanding the Monster in Your Family, in Your Office, in Your Bed—In Your World.* Riverhead Books, 2014.

Komrad, Mark S. MD. *You Need Help! A Step-by-Step Plan to Convince a Loved One to Get Counseling.* Hazelden Foundation, 2012.

Schouten, Ronald, MD, JD and Silver, James, JD. *Almost a Sociopath: Do I (Or Does Someone I Know) Have a Problem with Manipulation and Lack of Empathy?* Harvard University, 2012.